D0394516

"What an extremely exciting book this is! It feels like a missionary training manual to read as we are preparing for an overseas adventure. However, this time the world is not across the ocean, but right here where we live. Books like this give me hope for the future church—may we take what is written within these pages seriously."

Dan Kimball
Pastor, Vintage Faith Church
Author, *The Emerging Church*

"Once in a great while, a book comes along that (at least from some good vantage point) gives us a way to see the essence of something, and shows us essentially what we must do. Addressing the stagnation of traditional parish Christianity, this book does this, *and* it tells us why, and shows us how."

George G. Hunter III
Distinguished Professor of Evangelization
School of World Mission and Evangelization
Asbury Theological Seminary

"Dr. Ed Stetzer is a godly brother, dear friend, and the best missional thinker in North America. He and David Putman have given us a book that is desperately needed and essential reading for anyone desiring cultural transformation by Jesus through the church."

Mark Driscoll
Pastor, Mars Hill Church, Seattle
President, Acts 29 Church Planting Network

"Full of soul and missionary vision, *Breaking the Missional Code* will be a great handbook for the Christian Movement at the dawn of the 21st century. While grounded in the best thinking in terms of theory, it offers the best practice in terms of application. My bet is that it is going to prove indispensable for people and churches wanting to move towards adopting a genuinely missional stance in the West. I heartily recommend it."

Alan Hirsch
Director of Forge Mission Training Network
Author, *The Forgotten Ways: Reactivating the Missional Church*

"Ed Stetzer and David Putman have simply outdone themselves with this book. I read this book with enthusiasm from page one to the very last page. It is intertwined with principles that are real-time and taking place. We will recommend that all of our church planters and glocal pastors devour this book."

Bob Roberts
Senior Pastor NorthWood Church,
Author, *Transformation*

"This book is a must-read for anyone who wants to lead or participate in the transition from the program-driven model to a missional expression. Nobody gets it better than Ed. Now, because of his and David Putman's spot-on analysis and well-crafted suggestions, you can get it too! *Breaking the Missional Code* enables you to move past bewilderment so you can join the missional movement."

Reggie McNeal
Author, *The Present Future*

"Embrace the Jesus Call. Break the Missional Code for your community. Join God's Kingdom Expansion where God has planted you. *Breaking the Missional Code* will start you on that journey. Don't delay. The harvest is waiting."

Dave Travis
Executive Vice President, Leadership Network

"Ed Stetzer and David Putman challenge churches to look beyond prepackaged programs and marketing approaches to evangelization. The one-size-fits-all approach no longer works—if ever it did. Instead, they insist that we must think like missionaries in our own context. We must learn to observe and interpret our culture. They provide an antidote to the good news of Jesus Christ being rejected not because it is considered false but because it is deemed irrelevant. Here are valuable insights to help churches communicate the world's most vital message with clarity and power as a voice within the culture."

Eddie Gibbs
Author, *ChurchNext* and *Emerging Churches*

"*Breaking the Missional Code* is an important ground breaking book. It is the first book that discerningly applies international mission principles to North American contexts. It is a must read for any church serious about the Great Commission in North America and around the world."

Elmer Towns
Dean, Liberty University

"To remain biblically faithful and culturally relevant is a challenging mix. *Breaking the Missional Code* will help you navigate these uncharted waters and help your church connect with the vast number of people who are disconnected from God. This is a book your entire staff team needs to read and process together."

Bob Reccord
President, North American Mission Board

BREAKING

the missional

CODE

BREAKING
the missional
CODE

Your Church Can Become a
Missionary in Your Community

ED STETZER &
DAVID PUTMAN

BROADMAN
& HOLMAN
PUBLISHERS

NASHVILLE, TENNESSEE

Ten-Digit ISBN: 0-8054-4359-2
Thirteen-Digit ISBN: 978-0-8054-4359-2

Published by Broadman & Holman Publishers
Nashville, Tennessee

The graphic on technology and arts in worship services on
page 142 is used by permission of *OnMission,* a publication of
North American Mission Board.

Dewey Decimal Classification: 253.7
Subject Heading: EVANGELISTIC WORK /
PASTORAL THEOLOGY
Unless otherwise noted, Scripture quotations are from the Holy
Bible, New International Version, copyright © 1973, 1978, 1984 by
International Bible Society. Scriptures marked NKJV are from the
New King James Version, copyright © 1979, 1980, 1982, Thomas
Nelson, Inc., Publishers.

3 4 5 6 7 8 9 10 11 12 15 14 13 12 11 10 09 08 07 06

To my familiy: Tami, Dave, and Amanda, who have taught me a great deal on this journey. (David Putman)

To my family: Donna, Kristen, Jaclyn, and Kaitlyn, who are patient during the too-many nights that Dad is writing in the basement. Thanks, girls. (Ed Stetzer)

Contents

Introduction

ACROSS NORTH AMERICA, PASTORS AND churches are excited. Dynamic pastors are pioneering new methods and models to effectively reach their communities. Many churches are experiencing explosive growth because they are learning to connect with their communities. Pastors and churches are breaking the cultural codes of their communities. People are responding to biblically faithful and culturally relevant outreach.

At the same time, many other pastors are frustrated. They have attended the conferences, bought the tapes, and applied the strategies. However, they have not experienced the "promised" results. People in their communities are just not responding in the same way; they are not responding as the high-energy conference leader promised.

Why are some churches and pastors so effective and others are not? Often, both faithfully preach, teach, and reach out. Even pastors of similar ability and conviction sometimes find that their strategies work for one pastor but not for the other (or maybe they do connect for both of them, but surprisingly, they do not work for many others).

We are convinced that you can be equally called, gifted, and passionate and yet experience different levels of success due to the model of ministry being used. In other words, *the way you do things* does impact your ability to reach your community effectively. This book will assist you in being able to think through your context, apply universal principles in your mission setting, and then identify and apply strategies that will make you more effective in your context.

Breaking the code does not mean just finding the best model (or models) for your community. Instead, it means discovering the principles that work in every context, selecting the tools most relevant for your context (which may come from methods and models), and then learning to apply them in a missionally effective manner. It means thinking missiologically, and "if we are not focusing on missiology then we are being disobedient to the Great Commission."[1] According to Mittelberg, "For those of us who have our sights set on reaching secular people in our increasingly post-Christian society, we must step back and figure out what our mission field's cultural landscape looks like."[2]

Missionaries have known this for centuries. They know that they must have a profound understanding of their host culture before planning a strategy to reach the unique people group that exists in that cultural context. This is why they first study the culture to find strategies that will work among the people who live in that cultural setting. Missions history is filled with stories of great revivals because missionaries were able to "break the code," and the church exploded in their community. The missionaries found the redemptive window through which the gospel could shine.

For many, the idea that there is a missional code is odd. After all, they think, *This is not a mission field.* This may explain the way many church leaders distinguish evangelism from missions: evangelism takes place near us; missions take place overseas. Some churches are "far-thinking" and "far-reaching" about international missions but fail to reach the people in the shadows of their own steeples. This is because North America is often not seen as a mission field, or it is seen as a "reached" field only in need of an evangelism strategy. We tend to think that true missional engagement is not necessary in our paganized, secularized, spiritualized North American culture.

Evangelism is telling people about Jesus; missions involves understanding them before we tell them. No matter what you believe about the North American context—largely reached or unreached, religious hotbed or mission field, pagan or Christian—we can all agree that large segments of people in our society have not been reached. Many aspects of our culture have yet to be influenced with the gospel. Applying missionary principles in the North American context means that we seek to understand the cultural situation and its people as we seek to reach them with the gospel. That will allow all of us to be more effective as we join God in making more and better followers of Jesus Christ.

Moreover, what is really needed is not just an understanding of missiological thinking but a commitment to apply "missional" thinking as well. While missiology concerns itself with study *about* missions and its methodologies, missional thinking focuses on *doing* missions everywhere. It forces us to see our geographical context through the lenses of people groups, population segments, and cultural environments. An understanding of basic missiological thinking should prepare Christian leaders to be missional in their approach. We must ask: How can we teach our leaders to move beyond trying to recycle and reproduce church culture models and move toward a more biblical and missional approach in each of their unique cultural settings?

Today, we need to function as international missionaries have for centuries. Why? Because Scripture teaches that the church is God's missionary in the world. If we are going to join God on his mission, we have to recognize that we are missionaries . . . wherever he places us—just like the first disciples.

Chapter 1

The Emerging Glocal Context

"I remember being broken by the fact that there weren't too many churches reaching the next generation who were both post-modern and multi-ethnic in flavor. As a kid, my best friends were African-American or Caucasian. I had wondered why churches were so segregated. Furthermore, I saw how most of the churches I knew weren't connecting with my friends. Church seemed so irrelevant and boring to them."

David Gibbons, Newsong Church

BREAKING THE CODE REQUIRES A belief that there is a code to be broken. Breaking the code means that we have to recognize that there are cultural barriers (in addition to spiritual ones) that blind people from understanding the gospel. Our task is to find the right way to break through those cultural barriers while addressing the spiritual and theological ones as well.

That is what missionaries have always done. Today is no different. North America is a missions context, not because people are less Christian than they once were (although that is true), but because

God "sent" us to North America. It is a mission field because God sent us here as missionaries.

However, we are missing a clear reality if we do not recognize that this is a harder mission field than it once was. Historically, the Christian church was the first choice of spiritually minded North Americans—today, it often does not make the top ten list. Years ago, when people looked for spiritual answers, they looked to the church. Now, many look to anybody and anything but us.

Breaking the code is the recognition that there are visible and invisible characteristics within a community that will make its people resistant to or responsive to the church and its gospel message. Discerning Christians discover those relevant issues and break through the resistance—so that the name and reality of Jesus Christ can be more widely known.

One of the biggest cultural barriers we face is the emerging "glocal" context. We use this term to refer to the convergence of the **glo**bal reality with our lo**cal** reality. North America has become a "**glocal** community" requiring new strategies for effective ministry.

When the church was the first choice of spiritual seekers, we just needed to be there. They knew we were here. Most people had friends who attended. All they needed to do was come . . . and they did.

Now, we need more proactive strategies. We need to go to the people. Maybe we have lost ground because we have been thinking that they should just come to us. Now, we need methods and models that address the changing glocal context that is North America. People no longer think just locally; they think glocally.

First, it is important to understand the situation in which we find ourselves. A church that is a good example of living among cultural change is in Miami near Calle Ocho (Eighth Street), the center of what is now the Latino community. Calle Ocho was not always the center of Little Havana. At one time, it was part of the culture that existed in Miami before the Cuban influx.

Then, Batista fell and Castro came to power. One million Cubans moved into the neighborhood and, suddenly, that little church was no longer part of its community; it was a colony in the midst of another culture. It had to decide to change and reach its new neighbors or die. Like most churches, it chose to keep its culture and lose its community.

Today, the church in North America is in a similar situation. The culture has shifted. While this cultural shift has been more subtle and gradual than the one that took place in Miami, the cultural landscape has definitely changed. Lots of people throw terms around to describe the shift. The term that receives the most attention is "postmodernism." However, since postmodernism is an art form, a literary category, an academic discipline, and even a cultural force, even that fails to describe the situation. But, for the purpose of writing this book, we will use the term *postmodernism* to refer to the cultural shift that has taken place in our society. Many are now running from the term *postmodernism*. Since some have expressed concern about the influence of postmodernism in the emerging church, all books and topics that reference the word have to be hidden away! Yet until a new term arrives, we simply recognize that the world has changed and that we live in a world that has transitioned from the modern era to one that is "post."

Basically, postmodernity is the rejection of the modern view of life and the embracing of something new. It is not about GenXers (only pastors and marketers use that word now). For that matter, it is not really about postmodernism because while much of the culture has changed, it has not changed everywhere. This chart from *Planting New Churches in a Postmodern Age* will help illustrate the change in the broader culture from modernism to postmodernism and how it relates to the church.

The issue is that you have to decide where you are living. Are you in a community firmly entrenched in the worldview of modernity? If you seek to lead your church to reach postmoderns, you will first need to convert people to postmodernism and then to Christ. Is that really our mission?

Maybe you are in an area of the continent that is more comfortable with traditional approaches and churches. Great! Become

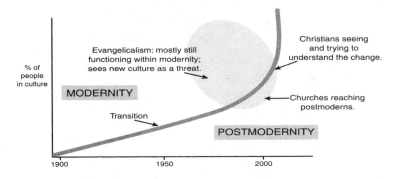

missional in that context, not a trendy community somewhere far away. For too many, they love their preferences and their strategies more than they love the people whom God has called them to reach.

We are sent as God's missionary.[1] The only question is where. "Just as God is a missionary God, so the church is to be a missionary church."[2] Jesus taught that "as the Father has sent me, I am sending you" (John 20:21). Our purpose, therefore, is to go to this new expression of life, culture, and values and to "face a fundamental challenge. That challenge is to learn to think about [our] culture in missional terms."[3]

Evangelicals have struggled with responding to these new realities, finding reasons not to respond. *It is important to note that the shift to postmodernism has not happened everywhere—it has not yet impacted many in the **church culture*** because the church culture acts as a protective shield, unmolested by a secular culture's music, literature, and values.

In large pockets of North America people still live each day in much the same manner as their parents before them. These people have more toys, but they still go to church (or at least feel guilty if they do not go), still have relatively stable family lives, and still espouse the "old values" of America. Most evangelicals live in these modern "pockets" of culture and have been somewhat insulated from the societal changes. Still, even though the societal shift has not yet made its fullest and deepest impact, many people can see the meteorite of cultural change moving their way. They can see the changes taking place in their children's lives—how they think and reason, how they view life, and how they act differently.

Evangelical churches, firmly rooted in modernity, sit in a culture that has moved beyond modern ideas. Language has changed, music has changed, and worldview has changed. Our churches need to decide whether they will be outposts of modernity in a new age or embrace the challenge of breaking a new cultural code.

Unchurched

Is there evidence that the culture has changed? Some churches are exploding, but most are not. For example, *the percentage of Christians in the U.S. population dropped 9 percent from 1990 to 2001.* The American Religious Identification Survey 2001, released by the Graduate Center of the City University of New York (CUNY) showed that the percentage proportion of Christians in the U.S. has declined—from 86 percent in 1990 to 77 percent in 2001.[4] Now, this refers to those people who claim to be Christians, from Howard Dean to George Bush. While it is fair to say that many who claim to be Christians do not know what it means to be one, still fewer people overall identify themselves as Christians.

George Barna tends to have a charitable definition for the unchurched. They are adults who have "not attended a Christian church service within the past six months, not including a holiday service (such as Easter or Christmas) or a special event at a church (such as a wedding or funeral)." Of course, a high percentage of people tend to indicate that they do attend church at least occasionally.

Even with Barna's charitable numbers, *the number of unchurched has almost doubled from 1991 to 2004.* A Barna Group study explained, "Since 1991, the adult population in the United States has grown by 15%. During that same period, the number of adults who do not attend church has nearly doubled, rising from 39 million to 75 million—a 92% increase!"[5]

Moreover, the number of "churched" people is much different from looking specifically at the number of evangelicals. In addition, evangelicals have obtained political power but exercise little moral influence. For many, evangelicals have become a voting block rather than a spiritual force.

Among evangelicals, true spiritual commitment seems to be lagging. For example, born-again church members divorce at a higher rate than the unchurched.[6] This lack of commitment may also be reflected in the fact that many so-called evangelicals decide to remain unchurched. According to *Christianity Today,* "The Barna Research Group reports that in the United States about 10 million self-proclaimed, born-again Christians have not been to church in the last six months, apart from Christmas or Easter."[7]

Although some churches have broken the code, in general, the church's influence is declining both in the culture and among its own people. Instead of biblical Christianity, spirituality appears to be the preferred "religion" of North America.

Gallup provides further insight in a January 2002 poll—50 percent of Americans described themselves as "religious," while another 33 percent said that they are "spiritual but not religious" (11 percent said neither and 4 percent said both).[8] A recent book, *Spiritual but Not Religious,* chronicles this growing trend.[9] Both the media and academia have firmly embraced and clearly promote the idea that spirituality is good and religion is bad.

This trend may explain why more students identify themselves as "no religion" rather than "Protestant" on college campuses.

Results from the Higher Education Research Institute at UCLA show that an equal number of incoming freshman in the fall of 2004 checked "None" as claimed "Protestant" on the question of religious identity. In total 28% identify themselves as Catholic, 17% say Protestant, 17% say "none," 11% say "other Christian," 4% Mormon, 4% Seventh Day

Adventist, 4% Unitarian, 3% Church of Christ, 3% "other religions," 2% Jewish, 1% each for Buddhist, Hindu, Islamic and Eastern Orthodox. (Spirituality Report, as reported in e-update #76)[10]

Ethnic Diversity

The growing number of unchurched people is just part of the story. The rest of the story is the growing diversity of North America. There was a day when a viable church in a community could be considered a major part of the solution. This is no longer true. Our growing cultural diversity requires a church within the reach of every people group, population segment, and cultural environment if we are to be faithful to the Great Commission. Dave Gibbons of Newsong Church understood this when he said:

> This idea of a new song started to align with a passage I had read earlier that year about new wineskins. I remember being broken by the fact that there weren't too many churches reaching the next generation who were both post-modern and multi-ethnic in flavor. As a kid, my best friends were African-American or Caucasian. I had wondered why churches were so segregated. Furthermore, I saw how most of the churches I knew weren't connecting with my friends. Church seemed so irrelevant and boring to them. Then I took a hard look at where I was serving. It was a great church yet because of its immigrant nature it was not reaching the new global village that was fast emerging. It became clear to me what the "new song" was. It was to begin a multi-ethnic movement that would reach the next generation."[11]

Dave is a pioneer in breaking the code among emerging multi-ethnic churches. Since launching Newsong in 1994 they have met in over thirty locations. They are made up of fifteen different ethnic groups, which are predominately Asian, ranging from Korean to Japanese. They also have a growing Hispanic and African-American population within the church. Like many churches out of the emergent vein they have a strong passion for global concerns, social justice, and advocating for the poor.[12] Newsong illustrates the growing complexity of reaching all people in North America.

I (David) will never forget meeting with a group of second-generation Koreans. Loyal by nature, they were greatly challenged by the need to plant the church among those who were born in a Korean family but raised in an American culture, speaking English as their primary language. Because of that dynamic, their language and experiences were radically different from that of their parents. In order for the gospel to be viable to their generation, they needed a church that spoke their cultural language.

Breaking the code is about seeing the unchurched through three different sets of lenses that include people groups, population segments, and cultural environments. It is about seeing that our work as the church is not completed until God's kingdom has come home to every tribe living within a given context.

People Groups

As more and more North Americans identify themselves with ethnic or national backgrounds, the story is about more than just the broader culture. Ethnic America does a tremendous job at revealing some telling trends. They correctly assert that this will be the "Ethnic Millennium." For example:

- In the 90s, while the general U.S. population grew by 6 percent, Asians grew by 107 percent, Hispanics grew by 53 percent, Native Americans grew by 38 percent.
- Twenty-five of the largest U.S. cities are now majority ethnic. Ethnics make up 61 percent of Chicago, 73 percent of New York, and 78 percent of Los Angeles.

- There are more Filipinos and Armenians in Los Angeles than in any city in the world. There are more Cubans in Miami than in Havana.[13]

Russell Begaye, cofounder of Ethnic America, explained: "We need to research the demographics, lifestyles and interests of the groups we want to reach. We need to go among the people, to make our message culturally relevant."[14] In other words, there is not just one white, young, emerging cultural code to be broken. The gospel needs to penetrate every culture . . . and every culture needs to be exegeted for the gospel.

Population Segments

In addition to the many unreached people groups or ethnic groups that now call North America home, people can be identified and segmented into many population segments. While people groups represent the largest common denominator among ethnic groups, a common language helps establish unique cultural influences within a context that certain groups share and enhances a sense of community.

Some missiologists and researchers use psychographics to help them understand how people relate and what binds them together. "Psychographics is a system for measuring consumers' beliefs, opinions and interests. It's like demographics but instead of counting age, gender, race, etc., it counts psychological information (opinions on abortion, religious beliefs, music tastes, personality traits, etc.). Marketing research usually combines demographic and psychographic information."[15] While this may be helpful in understanding social behavior, it can also be far too complex in reality. Simply put, people are bound by common experience. It is this common experience, when significant enough, that becomes a foundation for long- term social bonding and interaction. Therefore a population segment may consist of second generation Asians, young urban runaways, factory workers, parents of sports-active children, former addicts, wealthy Anglo professionals, divorced mothers with preschoolers, cowboys, victims of crime, skate boarders, etc. When their common experience is significant enough to impact values, belief and lifestyle, a new tribal community comes into existence, creating the opportunity to impact this very unique population segment when the code is broken. Where this code has been broken it is not unusual to see cowboy churches, biker churches, recovery churches, and the likes emerge.

Cultural Environments

In addition to people groups and population segments we must also consider cultural environments as part of our missionary mandate if the gospel is to be planted effectively among all people. Just as language and experience can define one's cultural preferences, geographical environments can serve as the common bond that brings people together. Today we are seeing more and more collegiate churches planted among the universities and colleges of North America. Prior to this decade one would have been hard pressed to find a church on a college campus—mainly because the code since the "Jesus Movement" has been translated into campus ministries established as an extension of certain denominations or parachurch ministry.

Jaeson Ma is a code breaking leader who established Campus Church Networks as a house church network designed to establish churches on and around college campuses. Jaeson was deeply burdened when he discovered that he was one of two Christians in a Philosophy 101 class. After beginning to prayer walk he began to see many doors open on the 28,000-student campus. After seeing many of the students come to know Christ he realized that very few of them were assimilated into a local church and that very few of the churches were prepared to minister to the college students.

After studying the Chinese model of underground house church, "he realized that a church could be planted on a college campus if a trained missionary could pray and win a student of peace or natural leader for Christ. The missionary would then teach the student leader to win his network of friends and from that network of friends start a small church. Once started, the missionary would then model for and disciple the natural student leader of the group on how to pastor the church with the goal of one day releasing him/her to actually be the pastor and train him/her to raise up their own student leaders to start other churches."[16] Jaeson went on to plant a house church network on the San Jose University, but God used Jaeson to help start a movement of campus churches around the world.

Collegiate churches serve as only one example of what it means to break the code among cultural environments. There are many geographical environments around North America where the code is being broken or needs to be broken, which include multihousing units, nursing homes, prisons and jails, factories, offices complexes, etc.

A New Reality

The reality is that we are now global and local, at the same time. Some have speculated, and we think it probably is true, that North America is the most diverse nation in the world. Though nobody knows the exact number, hundreds of languages are spoken across this continent. This should clearly illustrate our need to live within the glocal context that already exists.

Being in a glocal context should cause us to think, speak, and act differently. In addition, we must recognize that while the broader culture has changed, most evangelical churches have not. The broader culture has "shifted," and hundreds of new cultures have emerged within the existing cultural milieu. It is time for the North American church to enter its emerging glocal context.

It may sound uncharitable, but we don't mean it to be so. But . . . many will say that these shifts, and a book like this, do not matter. They are convinced if you just "preach the gospel" and perhaps "love people" that your church will reach people. They are wrong, and their ideas hurt the mission of the church. Communities across North America are filled with churches led by loving gospel preachers—most of whom, if statistics are true, are not reaching people.

You cannot grow a biblically faithful church without loving people and preaching the gospel. But loving people means understanding and communicating with them. Preaching the gospel means to proclaim a gospel about the Word becoming flesh—and proclaiming that the body of Christ needs to become incarnate in every cultural expression.

The Breaking the Code Challenge

1. Describe the specific people groups, population segments, and/or cultural environments that make up your geographical context.
2. What are some practical ways you can begin to expose those you minister with to opportunities to break the code?
3. How would you define success when it comes to the Great Commission in your given context?

Chapter 2

Breaking the Missional Code

"I know you don't want to talk to me, but can I bribe you with a little Starbucks."

Kevin Sullivan, High Pointe Church

IT TOOK MONTHS OF BUILDING a relationship, but my (David's) neighbor Rick finally showed up at church. At the time the church was meeting in an old movie theater. As Rick was greeted that morning, it was obvious that he was out of his comfort zone. With sweat beading up on his forehead he nervously asked, "Where do I pay?" He received a reassuring response: "Rick, it's free. Relax and enjoy your experience. We are so glad you came."

Rick represents a growing number of people born in North America who have no Christian memory. There is no doubt that the landscape has radically changed, as Dorothy puts it in the *Wizard of Oz,* "We are not in Kansas anymore." The spiritual landscape of North American culture is falling apart and coming together again at the same time. Spirituality is up, while church attendance is at an all-time low. It is commonly reported that at least 80 percent of churches have either plateaued or are in serious decline. Yet some churches that dot our landscape are experiencing phenomenal success and significance. Len Sweet explains it this way: "The movement of God is like a tornado, if we could only learn to connect the dots."

Breaking the code is about connecting the dots. Breaking the code is good news for any church committed to rethinking its mission and ministry. It answers the question, "Why are certain churches and ministries experiencing phenomenal success and massive growth in the midst of the apparent crisis within the North American church?"

Like tornadoes, many code-breaking churches are having a phenomenal impact. They dot the North American landscape. Here are a few that we have observed up close.

Mars Hill Church, Seattle, Washington

Mark Driscoll planted Mars Hill Church ten years ago. He had no seminary education and no pastoral experience, just a hunger to reach out to urban Seattle. The church had no direct mail strategy, no high-visibility location, and no television ministry. Yet ten years later the church averages five thousand in the most unchurched city in North America.

Mars Hill Church has also helped launch a movement of new churches through Acts 29, a church planting organization that Mark cofounded (and where Ed serves as a board member). The church has been written about widely and even appeared in a documentary broadcast on all ABC television affiliates.

What happened?

Mountain Lake Community Church, Cumming, Georgia

Mountain Lake Community Church was planted by Shawn Lovejoy in 2000. It is located just north of Atlanta (and where David serves as a founding member and now one of the pastors). In 2000 it started in a primary school cafeteria with a handful of mostly unchurched people. From the primary school, the church moved into a high school, where it grew to nearly five hundred in worship attendance. After moving into its first building (built to accommodate approximately 500 adults and children), the worship attendance exploded to nearly two thousand in less than two years.

What happened?

Set Free Church, Yucaipa, California

We have watched Set Free Church in Yucaipa, California, over the past decade with amazing interest. When we first began to take note of the church, Pastor Willie Dalgity had just acquired a church building where another church group had disbanded. He had gathered about two hundred former bikers, addicts, and homeless people and launched their first daughter church in an old Harley-Davidson shop in San Bernardino.

Five years later, the congregation had outgrown its facilities and was moving into a new facility large enough for a thousand. In addition, they had launched some twenty-seven daughter churches in the Los Angeles area, along with a number of churches in Seattle and Atlanta. In ten years they have started some forty churches. As we write, Set Free is exploring other options to begin ministries in Las Vegas, Philadelphia, and New York City.

What happened?

Saddleback Community Church, Mission Viejo, California

Who would have known that in just over two decades Saddleback Church would be near 20,000 in attendance, and Pastor Rick Warren would be known around the world as the author of *The Purpose*

Driven Church and *The Purpose Driven Life?* As part of Saddleback's explosive growth "more than 320,000 pastors and church leaders from over 120 countries have attended Purpose-Driven Church seminars in 18 languages, and tens of thousands of churches have adopted the PDC strategy."[1] In addition they have started dozens of daughter churches and sent approximately five thousand of their members around the world.

What happened?

Northwood Church, Keller, Texas

Northwood Church was planted by Bob Roberts. Over the past fifteen years, it has grown to over two thousand in attendance while planting eight churches within two miles of their main campus. On any given Sunday, over five thousand people are in worship within this two-mile radius as a result of their efforts. In addition to this local growth, they have planted over fifty-seven churches, with another nineteen scheduled to be planted this year. Recently, this group of daughter and granddaughter churches has joined together to form GlocalNet, a group of churches committed to seeing the first global church-planting movement by planting churches around them and around the world. As a result of this network, over one hundred churches per year will be planted around the world.

What happened?

Awakening Chapels

Neil Cole, founder of Church Multiplication Associates, began planting Awakening Chapels in Long Beach, California. He focused on reaching out relationally to those disconnected from Christ in an urban coffeehouse setting. His goal has been to see disciples and churches reproducing quickly. By the end of 1999 there were nine Awakening Chapel churches; by the end of 2000 there were fifty!

From 2000 till 2005, three hundred more relation-based churches have been planted "with the number now doubling each year. These churches focus on small, communal, reproducible structures and target unreached 'pockets of people,' mostly in America's southwest."[2]

What happened?

First Baptist, Woodstock, Georgia

For its first 150 years, Woodstock's First Baptist Church was like most country churches. That changed when Johnny Hunt became pastor in 1986. He emphasized preaching, visitation, and Sunday school. When he came, attendance was around two hundred. We've both "sat under Johnny's preaching," and it is a cultural site to behold! Johnny is an enthusiastic country preacher (lots of yellin' and stompin' and sweatin') who presents a clear and compelling message—and thousands come to Christ each year. He has broken the North Georgia cultural code, and he is effectively reaching the unchurched, both in the upper and lower socioeconomic strata.

Since Johnny's arrival, Woodstock has grown over 1,300 percent and recently completed an 8,000-seat auditorium. Their 13,500 membership is larger than the city of Woodstock. The church is consistently one of the top 100 churches in baptisms within their denomination. They offer many outreach-oriented ministries for the unchurched in their community, have planted a number of significant churches, have a variety of compassion ministries, and have an incredible global impact through their mission efforts.

What happened?

A New Breed

Each one of these leaders represents a new breed of pastors in North America who see their context through missional lenses. They have the ability to read the culture and translate ministry into a biblically faithful and culturally appropriate expression of church.

Many churches that break the code will look similar—particularly if they are in similar areas. There is nothing wrong with learning from other churches. What is different is the process.

Sometimes a pastor will get excited about a model or a method learned at a conference. Then the pastor will come home and import that model into the community. Sometimes it works; sometimes it doesn't. Most of the time, it does not work as well. Why? Because the methods and models that God uses in one place does not mean he will use them in another place. The fact that a missional breakthrough occurred in Seattle does not mean that God will use the same methods in Sellersburg, Indiana.

Here is a better process to learn from others:

1	2	3	4	5
Calling from God	→ Exegeting the community	→ Examining ways God is working in similar communities	→ Finding God's unique vision for your church	→ Adjusting that vision as you learn the context

Calling from God

Any genuine attempt at missional effectiveness begins with a calling from God. We have already explored some of what that involves. Above all else, we need to be called by God to a certain people. There may be a unique calling to "the ministry," but there certainly is a call to people. The call to people is essential because it helps us escape the trap of technique.

We love technique. Technique is not all bad, but our uncritical dependence on it can be. It is a North American cultural value; we want to find something that works so we can apply it "here." We want success. We want to be as successful as others who have applied the techniques. Those who have been successful want to share their techniques (it seems that few people want to go to a conference to hear about praying to find God's unique call for your church). We value technique, and sometimes it keeps us from hearing God's voice and vision regarding our church.

Our first task is to listen for God's call to us, not to respond to his call to others.[3] He first calls us to an intimate relationship to himself. Only after fully engaging in that relationship will he reveal his plan for ministry to us. Many church planters, pastors, and various leaders simply seize the first "cool" model that comes along and attempt to make it fit into their communities. All the while, many decry the use of similar methods by others in the community because they are not as "hip."

The key to breaking the code of a community is to have the heart of the Father for that community. The only way to do that is by spending serious amounts of time with the one who loved Jerusalem deeply enough to weep over it. We must have that same weeping spirit for the lost of our own glocal communities.

Perhaps our greatest fault is that we use a nebulous urgency for pressing ahead before we have heard from God. We have the callings of God to witness and compassionately care for the lost. And we should practice those things and teach our people to do the same. The fault occurs when we launch a new model, employ a new worship style, and try to break the code before we have sufficiently heard from the one who wrote the original human code.

We then move to the call of God *to someone*. Jesus said, "As the Father has sent me, I am sending you" (John 20:21). To be sent from God (like Jesus) requires us to be sent somewhere and to someone. John Knox expressed it well when he said, "Give me Scotland or I die." He was not sent to France or Belgium. God gave him a passion for the Scottish people.

Missionaries have known this for centuries: To reach a tribe we must first have a call to reach them, and then have a love for the people. We need to receive God's call and have a love for that group.

That love becomes the force that overcomes the lure of technique. As much as we might love the great things that God is doing in Dallas or Atlanta, as much as we might wish that we could be as influential as that pastor in Seattle or Orlando, and as much as we might wish our church was as avant garde as the "famous" churches, we must love the people enough to build a church that breaks the code in the community to which God has called us!

So breaking the code begins with asking God, "Who have you called me to?" Perhaps you have never asked this question, "God, who is it you are calling me to reach?" Until we are prepared to answer this question, we should go no further. As we open our eyes and view the harvest, we might be surprised. When we answer that question, we can begin to move toward becoming that missional church that breaks the code. The journey is just beginning.

Exegeting the Community

Rick Warren, perhaps the most famous missional code breaker, surveyed his community and found why people in his community did not go to church. He found that there were four primary complaints about church:

1. Church is boring, especially the sermons. The messages don't relate to my life.
2. Church members are unfriendly to visitors. If I go to church, I want to feel welcomed without being embarrassed.
3. The church is more interested in my money than it is in me.
4. We worry about the quality of our church's childcare.[4]

So Warren developed his strategy from an analysis of the community. Since people had four common complaints, he determined to try to address those concerns in his outreach. Warren then sent out a letter that explained why people did not attend church and what they might expect to experience at Saddleback. He sent a letter into his community announcing the launch of this new church. Under the section in the letter "why people don't attend church," Warren listed:

- The sermons are boring and don't relate to daily living
- Many churches seem more interested in your wallet than you
- Members are unfriendly to visitors
- You wonder about the quality of nursery care for your children.[5]

Warren then sent out a letter explaining why people did not attend church and what they might expect at Saddleback. In this letter he stated:

- Meet new friends and get to know your neighbors
- Enjoy upbeat music with a contemporary flavor
- Hear positive, practical messages that encourage you each week
- Trust your children to the care of dedicated nursery workers.[6]

Soon, people all over North America were using Warren's letter. They could do the math—send out 20,000 copies of Rick's magic letter and 200 people will come to the first service (full disclosure here—I [Ed] did it and had 234 people at our first service!). Here is the problem—the top four complaints that Warren built his strategy around are not the same complaints in your community.

Warren's process, not his letter, is the key. He asked the unchurched about their values, needs, and preferences and then developed his outreach strategy accordingly. We need to exegete our communities as well.

Pastors can exegete their communities and discover what their local objections are. They may be similar, but the further you are culturally from Warren's Southern California, the less similar the objections will be. In order to break the code, you must seek to understand the culture before you choose your model. As you decipher your own community, you may discover similar methods and models that have been used effectively in other like-minded communities.

Examine Ways God Is Working in Similar Communities

Perhaps the most significant untold story surrounding many of these churches is how God has used their new and emerging expressions of church to impact similar communities all around the country. If you examine the core of people within these churches, you will discover that those who make up the core of the church, from a demographical and psychographical perspective, are consistent with those who are outside the church. We have discovered that when the growing core of leaders, the pastoral leadership, and the community are from the same tribe, then the potential for impact is significant.

A second principle relates to the similarity of certain population segments from one geographical area to another. Saddleback is a good example. If you look at their demographics, you discover, as they did, a "Saddleback Sam" (see *The Purpose Driven Church*). Well, guess what? "Saddleback Sam" lives not only in Orange County, California but also in certain geographical contexts all over the country. Where you find "Saddleback Sam," you do not need to reinvent the wheel of how to do culturally relevant forms and expressions of ministry. Rick Warren did us a huge favor when he broke the code for Saddleback Sam. This explains why the Saddleback model has worked and not worked all over the country. Where you find a similar demographic with similar values and lifestyles, the Saddleback expression of church and ministry is likely to be successful. (Note that Rick Warren does not consider the Purpose Driven Church methodology to be a cultural expression. When we refer to the Saddleback model, we are not talking about the five purposes that drive the church but the style of Saddleback.[7])

We also see this principle in church expressions like Set Free, which we mentioned earlier. When they move into a new region or part of the country, they do not have to revamp their approach to starting and growing churches. They may have to adapt some aspects of their ministry, but the code has been broken.

A good example of this is found outside of Atlanta, Georgia, where Set Free has a growing network of ministries and churches. One of the key elements to their strategy in Yucaipa, California, is their ranches. The key to the strategy of Set Free was to provide a place where the addicts who have found Christ can get off drugs and begin intense discipleship. Thus, they have developed ranches out in the desert for that sole purpose. Outside of Atlanta in Gainesville, Georgia, Set Free has what they call a "farm." Ranches are farms—the difference is using language that is relevant to the Southeast.

Leaders and churches that have broken the code have great potential to multiply across the country among similar population segments. In other words, wherever there is a people group, population segment, or cultural environment that is like the original church or ministry, then the methods, models, and techniques are often transferable. In these cases, we need to connect the dots.

Find God's Unique Vision for Your Church

According to an article in *Christianity Today*, "God's kingdom is not best represented by franchises of McChurch. If you focus your energies on copying someone else's methodologies or programs, you will miss something crucially important . . . The Holy Spirit is empowering transformational leaders who demonstrate the kingdom of God in unique ways in each different community."[8]

Churches should function differently from location to location. When it comes to the kingdom of God, uniformity is not a value. Instead, Scripture speaks of and celebrates every tongue, tribe, and nation. The kingdom is not about individuals being processed into a monolithic kingdom of clones. Instead, it celebrates not only the individual but also his tongue and tribe. In other words, God is most glorified when the churches that honor him reflect the diversity of his vast kingdom.

When churches and leaders are open to creating visions, God gives direction and passion. National Community Church began in January 1996 with three people, Pastor Mark Batterson and his wife and son. The church grew to twenty or twenty-five over the next nine months. Beginning in a school, they were profoundly impacted by a sudden notification that they would have to leave. In God's providence they began meeting in a movie theater in Union Station just four blocks from the state capitol in November of that year. Today they average over nine hundred people each weekend. They meet in two different locations and offer four different services each week. Two of their services are live and two are via video venue. They are unique in that they rotate their live and video venues. Pastor Mark's vision flows out of a conviction that "God strategically positions us in the middle of the marketplace."[9] Part of the vision is to continue to multiple into other marketplaces and movie venues throughout Northern Virginia (see http://www.theaterchurch.com/).

Thus, every church must find its unique call and vision. Not every church is called to reach the same people, worship using the same music, attract the same people, and appreciate the same values. For most churches, this happens accidentally. The church takes on the character of its people—and in the process it often distances itself from the community. Churches that break the code seek to communicate the Word and connect through worship with local people and culture. This takes place as they enact God's vision for their local church. In the process, they develop a unique vision for their church that both honors God and connects with their community.

Adjusting Vision as You Learn the Context

I (Ed) recently consulted with a large and successful church in a Midwestern city. They had been planted in the early nineties, had grown to megachurch size, and by all outward indications were a strong church. Yet the pastoral leadership team invited me to consult with the church's key leaders because they were having little success reaching subsequent generations. They felt stuck.

The problem with determining a community's values and needs is that they change . . . but often the church does not. Understandably, this situation leads many to criticize cultural relevance. If a church spends all of its time trying to "keep up with the times," it may have difficulty "keeping up with" the Scriptures. As appealing as that argument might be on the surface, it quickly breaks down upon further, and more thorough, examination.

If a church does not regularly examine its culture, it ends up as a culture unto itself. Soon the church is filled with people who pray in King James English, call the pastor "brother" to show respect, and forbid women from wearing pants to church. They are still relating to cultural issues that were relevant one hundred years before. However, that culture and those issues have long since disappeared—everywhere, that is, except within the church. Instead, the church needs to regularly ask, "Are we faithfully proclaiming the faith in the place in which we find ourselves today?" A church will be completely faithful only when it is faithful to its God, its Scripture, and its mission in the world.

Conclusion

So breaking the code is missionary work, and it is best seen as a missions process. A commitment to the integrity and authority of Scripture, combined with a passion for reaching the people to whom you are called, requires a commitment to prayerfully create a plan and strategy to reach your community. New ways of thinking is the mandate—simply cloning other successful models is unlikely to work. In the next chapter, we will discuss several shifts that must take place toward missional ministry in churches that want to break the code.

The Breaking the Code Challenge

1. Describe the specific people that God has called you to reach.
2. Identify other churches that are being used by God to reach similar people.
3. Write a brief paragraph on what your church would look like if it broke the code among that people.
4. Identify the adjustments you need to make in light of what you are learning.

Chapter 3

Responding to the Commissions of Jesus

"My personal calling from God is to ministry focused on reaching non-believers to literally go where the [non-believers] are and sometimes do what they do. . . . Now they come to our church. They're willing to be baptized; they're willing to hear the gospel; they want to know more about Jesus Christ . . . . That only happened through our positive relationships. That's the approach that we take."
Christopher Jun, Joyful Life Church, Seattle, Washington

WHEN YOU CONSIDER HOW THE disciples scattered and hid surrounding the events of Jesus' crucifixion, his words to them—"make disciples of all nations"—don't seem to make much sense. How would this group of disciples find the inner strength to pull together and accomplish a missions task of local, much less worldwide, dimension and scope? How could this group who had publicly denied Jesus now proclaim with boldness him and his message of repentance and forgiveness? How could Jesus communicate with them in such a way that their lives would be transformed to the point of embracing this mission with all of their heart, soul, mind, and strength?

The answers to these questions are important because the church in North America appears to have forgotten its mission and its message. Many churches are struggling to break the code; they seem simply to be trying to satisfy their own preferences. This is a long way from Jesus' intent.

Jesus gave four directives that outline the missional mandate of the church. They challenge his followers with the call to be on mission, and they serve as the instruction manual for missional ministry. Each time Jesus gave a sending command, it was spoken to a group of his disciples. These same commands are still in effect for the church today, his current disciples.

We Are Sent (John 20:19–21)

> On the evening of that first day of the week, when the disciples were together, with the doors locked for fear of the Jews, Jesus came and stood among them and said, "Peace be with you!" After he said this, he showed them his hands and side. The disciples were overjoyed when they saw the Lord. Again Jesus said, "Peace be with you! As the Father has sent me, I am sending you."

The first passage including Jesus' sending commands begins by pointing out that the disciples were behind closed doors, and many churches still are today. Before sending them out, he saw them behind the locked door and gave a promise of peace. The promise of peace was critical. Disciples faced the challenge to move from hiding to engaging their community for the sake of the gospel. They were gripped by fear, but Jesus said, "Here is my peace. Go! Share it with others."

He reminded them in John 20:20 of his crucifixion: "He showed them his hands and side. The disciples were overjoyed when they saw the Lord." Then he reminded them again about his peace in verse 21. Jesus said, "Peace be with you!" Jesus proclaimed peace, reminded them of his crucifixion, pronounced peace again, and then told them, "As the Father has sent me, I am sending you" (John 20:21).

With that one command Jesus announced two thousand years of direction for the church, still in effect for the churches of today—even your church. He proclaimed that we are sent. The church is, and you are individually, God's missionary to the world. Your church is God's instrument to reach the world, and it includes reaching your community. We are *sent on mission* by God. We are to be a missional church by calling, nature, and choice. We are called to be on mission in our community. We have been sent to be on mission in our context, and we must accept that call, that directive to *be on mission* where God has placed us—not five, not fifty, not five hundred years ago and not thirty miles away, not three hundred miles away, not three thousand miles away. We are exhorted to be on mission where God has placed us *now*, and our job is to "break the code" wherever we are.

Being a code-breaking church means that often we are called to engage a culture that is not our own preferred culture. Our job is to take the gospel to each community, not hold on to our preferences. In addition, we can learn a lot about breaking codes from international missions. Let me (Ed) illustrate from a recent experience in Africa.

When you're a foreign leader visiting a church in Africa, you stand out. I visited one church in West Africa—one thousand Africans and me. They were singing and dancing—that is about as normal in church there as yelling "amen" in certain churches in the rural South. Then came the offering time . . . which is handled a little differently in Africa. They placed a big barrel in the front of the church, and all of a sudden one thousand people started getting up and dancing their way down the aisle in a conga line to drop their offerings in the barrel.

I was raised in the seventies, and the only way I knew how to dance was by pointing my fingers. So I started working/dancing my way down the aisle as best I could, gave my offering, came back, sat down, and thought to myself, *I didn't enjoy that.* Then it hit me . . .

I wonder if the missionaries who lived there enjoy that. For that matter, how about the pastors in North America who are called to different places and challenged to do some things that they might not enjoy—how do they feel?

Missions makes this point: it is not about us and our preferences. It is about *his mission* and the fact that he sends us. We want to practice our preferences. We want things to be the way we like them. But God wants us to be on mission with him, to be sent to some group of people somewhere, and to minister in a way that meets their needs, not promotes our preferences. When we are functioning as God's church sent on mission, we will go into different cultures, contexts, and communities. We will proclaim a faithful gospel there in a culturally relevant way, and we will worship in a way that connects in that setting. When the connection is made, the code is broken. God does not tell us that we will always like it. He does say that we *always* need to function as his missionary church.

This tension is not new. We find the early church struggling with many of the same issues. For Peter it was the issue of going to the Gentiles and eating meat. "The apostles and the brothers throughout Judea heard that the Gentiles also had received the word of God. So when Peter went up to Jerusalem, the circumcised believers criticized him and said, 'You went into the house of uncircumcised men and ate with them'" (Acts 11:1–3). It is not simply a tension we experience from those without, but it is also a tension we feel within as Peter continued to explain his action. After describing how he had heard the voice commanding him to go to the Gentiles, he stated, "I replied, 'Surely not, Lord! Nothing impure or unclean has ever entered my mouth'" (Act 11:8). You can see the tension that existed both from within and without. Breaking the code can be challenging.

In generations past this was less of an issue. Most Americans (at least of the Anglo variety) looked and thought somewhat alike. Similar to a pancake, the surface of the North American culture was flat and similar. Today, North America is like a waffle. If you hold a waffle flat, it looks like many evangelical churches. For many

Christians in their churches, everything looks the same . . . because they are living in an evangelical subculture.

Many evangelicals live in a "Christianized" world where people listen to James Dobson tell us how to raise our children, consult Ron Blue to understand our finances, sing along with Third Day for musical inspiration, choose political candidates based upon Christian Coalition voting guides, and read Tim LaHaye to enjoy some good Christian fiction. We live in this evangelical subculture, this evangelical bubble, and we see all kinds of people just like us. Some call this the "herding effect."[1] When you are running in the middle of a herd of buffalo, everything looks identical. What we see becomes our reality. We think that everyone around us knows where we are, and they can come to the church if they want to be like us.

When we turn up the waffle, we see a different picture. We see that the waffle is made up of multiple divots. These divots represent customs, cultures, communities, and contexts where people live out their lives with different preferences and worldviews—right next to mine. But until we embrace the words of Jesus, "As the Father has sent me, I am sending you," we will never truly embrace the missional mandate and become a church that breaks the code.

To All Kinds of Peoples

> Then Jesus came to them and said, "All authority in heaven and on earth has been given to me. Therefore go and make disciples of all nations, baptizing them in the name of the Father and of the Son and of the Holy Spirit, and teaching them to obey everything I have commanded you. And surely I am with you always, to the very end of the age" (Matt. 28:18–20).

In John 20:21, Jesus pronounced that we are sent. But it does not end there. He has given us more detail. In Matthew 28:18–20, Jesus gave another directive to his disciples. He stated, "All authority has been given to Me in heaven and earth (NKJV)." He set the stage by emphasizing his authority. After announcing his authority, though, he did not say, "Make sure all of your needs are met" or "Make sure all of your preferences are satisfied." What he said was, "Go therefore and make disciples of all nations."

In the Greek, the words for "all nations" are *panta ta ethnē*. We get our English word *ethnic* from the Greek word *ethnē*. When we hear (or read) Jesus' command to "go to all nations," we think countries. But when Jesus spoke those words, there were no countries as we understand them today. The nation-state is an invention of the modern era. In Jesus' day there were groups of people, and there were empires. Jesus' instructions mean that we must go to all the people groups in the world.

The Jewish disciples of that day knew that Jesus was speaking about the Gentiles. The gospel was to go beyond the Jewish nation. But they also thought of Phoenicians, Macedonians, Greeks, Romans, and others Jesus did not use the word for *empires* like the Roman Empire, the Persian, or the Greek. Jesus used the word for *peoples,* and the Jews knew this meant all the different kinds of Gentiles. It meant to go to *all* the different kinds of people that existed. This is still God's plan today.

In today's world, we have to remember that we are still sent . . . to all different kinds of peoples. The word *peoples* represents every ethno-linguistic people group around the world, all the different ethnicities present in our cities, and even the different generations that live in our communities. The divots of the waffle in which they live may be different from the one in which we live.

Jesus recognized that all the different kinds of people need the gospel. A couple of examples will illustrate this point. When I was a professor at Southern Seminary in Louisville, Kentucky, I trained church planters to plant churches among different kinds of people. One of my students, Daniel Montgomery, planted a church named Sojourn. Daniel asked me to fill in one Sunday when he was out of town.

Sojourn meets only on Sunday nights. As I walked into the church about ten minutes early, I noticed a couple of things. First, the band was warming up, and I immediately noticed that the music was way too loud. Second, I noticed that everybody was dressed "badly." They all had on black T-shirts and jeans. Most had weird hair, kind of spiked up, and it all looked messy. Now, I am not that old (thirty-eight), and I have planted contemporary churches my entire life. Even though I was actually only a few years older and ethnically similar to many of them, we were radically different.

The church is in a part of Louisville called "The Highlands." In this area, there are many artists/waiters. They are all trying to break through into whatever it is that art people break into professionally. They wear black; they are very serious-looking; and they look like they just came from a sculpting competition. Lots of people in the church had tattoos and facial jewelry—hooks, studs, and chains—it looked like half of them had fallen into a tackle box, gotten up, and just showed up at church like that.

After I preached, I went and sat in the back and watched. I watched as the church worshiped and prayed together in a community where most of the other churches had died out. Yet this church was two years old, and over two hundred people were attending. All around me were people who would never go to the churches that I pastored. Prior to Sojourn, they were not even going to the other churches in their own community. Even the church where they met, with its gothic look and oak walls, was no longer reaching its community. But Sojourn was now.

The service included lit candles and an indie rock musical feel. It was a fascinating service . . . but I didn't enjoy it very much. I didn't know many of the songs and could not sing along. The church had many people who wrote their own songs, and they were composed with the people of that community of faith in mind. This setting was definitely not my style.

When I went and sat in the back after preaching, the associate pastor, Les, served the Lord's Supper. He encouraged the people, "If you haven't committed your life to Christ, this isn't for you. If you've got unrepented sin, this isn't for you." About half of the people started coming forward, but half of them stayed in their seats. I was sitting in the back watching, and as the participants were coming back to their seats, they went to the people who had not gone forward and began to pray with them. All around me, just a few rows up, people began to weep, praying and crying out to God. They began to sing, and they began to worship with people on their knees.

These were people who dressed differently, people who liked different music, and people who had a different culture than me. But they were all worshiping the same Christ. I did not relate well to the context; it was not my preference. But it was not about me—God was there, and this was a holy place because somebody had followed the command of Jesus when he said, "As the Father has sent me, I am sending you . . . to all different kinds of peoples" (John 20:21; Matt. 28:18–20).

Daniel Montgomery said, "I'll go to these people and proclaim a faithful gospel there." The amazing thing is that a few years ago Daniel looked and acted a lot like me. He was willing to do whatever it took to break the code and reach this unique group of people. It was just different from the group God sent me to.

At the end of the day, I have to remember—we all have to remember—that it is not about me, it is not about you. It is about Jesus sending us to peoples to proclaim the gospel in a way that they can understand. Our churches often struggle because we put our preferences over our call—our preferences over our mission.

Soon after speaking at Sojourn, I was asked to preach in the evening service at a church in a blue-collar section of Oklahoma City. My plane was a few minutes late, so we got to the church about 6:10. They had already started. As I walked in late, I heard them singing the one form of music that God could never use—country/western. They were singing "Victory in Jesus," which is the Baptist National Anthem, but they were singing it in a unique way. It went like this: *"I heard an old, old story how a Savior came from glory—yeehaw."*

In addition, I noticed something strange about the way people were seated. There was a person, then a space, then a person, then a space. When I got closer, I saw it was a person and a cowboy hat and another person and a cowboy hat. As a boy who grew up in New

York City, I was a stranger in a strange land. I got up to preach. I was preaching as best I could, but they were yelling at me. I'd start talking about something the Lord was doing, and someone would yell at me, "Preach it, brother!" I said, "I'm trying—stop yelling at me!" They sang some more, and every once in a while, someone would just go "Yeehaw!"

So I preached, or they preached, or we preached together. There were a lot of people preaching that night. Afterwards we went to Ryan's—it's Oklahoma City—it's the law. I sat across the table from one of the men attending that church and asked, "Bob, what brought you to the church?" He said, "Preacher, six months ago I got out of prison" (he had my full attention at that moment), "and I went to one church, but I couldn't afford to buy the clothes like they wore, and I couldn't afford to go to the places they went to fellowship. Then I went to another church, and no one would accept me because of my background. Then I came to this church, and here six months ago, I got radically saved and washed in the blood."

I thought to myself, *I don't know if I can handle the culture. But this was a holy place—God was here.* And then God convicted me—It is not about me! They were exactly what God wanted them to be to reach this lower middle class, blue-collar community on the far side of Oklahoma City. Sojourn was exactly what God wanted them to be, and I knew that in both places there were empty church buildings all around them who said, "We've got our preferences, and we're here; ya'll come." These two churches decided to decipher their communities and proclaim a faithful gospel there. These two churches decided to be obedient to Jesus, who said, "As the Father has sent me, so send I you . . . to all different kinds of people groups."

Just as these two churches were faithful to go to their communities, we must be faithful to go to our communities. In today's context that means seeing our *panta ta ethnē* (all nations) through missional lenses. No longer can we see them simply through the lenses of ethno-linguistic people groups, but we must adjust our sight to see them through the lenses of people groups, population segments, and cultural environments. No longer can we assume that because two people are Anglo or Hispanic that they are the same *panta ta ethnē*.

There are huge differences from one group to the other, even those who often share the same ethnicity. In breaking the code it is important to make the following distinctions:

- *People groups.* Ethno-linguistic people groups—those who share the same ethnicity, language, and culture.
- *Population segments.* Subgroups within a distinct people group or at times may cross through several people groups, but share the same language and culture. For example, second-generation Koreans may share more in common with their postmodern Anglo neighbor living in downtown Seattle then with their first-generation parents living in San Francisco. A population segment could be a group of cowboys living in Oklahoma mentioned above.
- *Cultural environments.* Subgroups that are defined by a geographical environment. For example, those who are incarcerated in a local prison or university students living on a college campus.

With a Message

> He told them, "This is what is written: The Christ will suffer and rise from the dead on the third day, and repentance and forgiveness of sins will be preached in his name to all nations, beginning at Jerusalem. You are witnesses of these things" (Luke 24:46–48).

Jesus spoke again to his disciples and, by extension, to us as his church. With this he gave the clearest expression of the purpose of the commission. It is not about style; it is not about the externals; it is not about the culture. We have been called, commissioned, and consecrated to begin that journey personally and together with others in our church families. Jesus said that we are sent to all peoples, and we are sent with a message.

We are to be witnesses who proclaim this special message. This idea of God's people being witnesses emerges from the Old Testament. Isaiah 43:9–10 says, "All the nations gather together and the peoples assemble . . . You are my witnesses, declares the LORD." These verses clearly reveal that it is God's desire for his people to be his witnesses to all the people of the earth. God has always sought to gather people who would wholeheartedly give themselves to him, be his witnesses, and proclaim his message.

Here is the message—"repentance and forgiveness of sins to be preached in his name to all nations." When it becomes something other than repentance and forgiveness, then the gospel itself is lost in the process. When we forget that the job of the church is to proclaim the message of repentance and forgiveness of sins, the future of any church is bleak. We need to be reminded every day through God's Word, "As the Father has sent me, I am sending you . . . to every people group . . . with a message." The only question is—Will we be faithful to respond? We are sent as missionaries, the only question is—Are we good ones?

Empowered by the Spirit

> So when they met together, they asked him, "Lord, are you at this time going to restore the kingdom to Israel?" He said to them: "It is not for you to know the times or dates the Father has set by his own authority. But you will receive power when the Holy Spirit comes on you; and you will be my witnesses in Jerusalem, and in all Judea and Samaria, and to the ends of the earth" (Acts 1:6–8).

In the book of Acts, Jesus gave his last clear directive while on earth. He spoke to his disciples and, by extension, to all of his followers throughout history. When they met together, the disciples asked Jesus, "Lord, have you read the latest installment of the *Left Behind* series?"

Take a moment and look at Acts 1:6. Is that a fair paraphrase? I think it is. Look at what it says. Here they are two thousand years ago, and they are saying, "Lord, is this it? Is the rapture coming? Are you going to restore your kingdom to Israel?" Two thousand years later and evangelicals are still obsessed with the question.

Nothing is wrong with speculative fiction, but here is the point. Two thousand years ago the disciples said to Jesus, "Jesus, we want to know more about the end times." Here is Jesus' response (v. 7), "It is not for you to know the times or dates the Father has set by his own authority." When the disciples had an inordinate interest in the end times, much like we do today in North America among evangelicals, Jesus said, "Do not get focused on that!"

Instead, he said in verse 8, "But you will receive power when the Holy Spirit comes on you; and you will be my witnesses in Jerusalem, and in all Judea and Samaria, and to the ends of the earth." If only God's people would spend as much time and money learning how to be witnesses as they do reading a fiction series on the end times, then maybe we would not be living on the only continent in the world where the church is not growing.

We have become fascinated with the very things that Jesus said not to worry about. We have forgotten the things we are to be focused on, being the people whom he has sent in the power of his Spirit to reach out to all peoples with a profound message: "But you will receive power when the Holy Spirit comes on you; and you will be my witnesses in Jerusalem, and in all Judea and Samaria, and to the ends of the earth."

When I (Ed) was teaching at the seminary, I had the privilege of serving a small church named Rolling Fields Church. There were thirty-five people in the church, mostly senior adults. They called me and said, "Dr. Stetzer, we want you to come over and preach for us." I went.

It was a fascinating church. The median age was sixty-eight. They had a member named Greg who was in his thirties, and he was basically the youth group. The church leaders asked, "Dr. Stetzer, we want you to teach us how to reach our community." The problem was that their community had transitioned to become primarily young and ethnically diverse. It was not the same community that existed when they started the church in 1952.

I looked out at this congregation of thirty-five people with their oxygen tanks and walkers (I am exaggerating!), and I thought to myself, "You've got a long way to go in order to reach this community. It's going to be hard to reach the first person, much less the second one." People were going to visit this church and say, "Is there anyone here like me? Do I feel welcome here?"

Over a period of time, the church said, "We can do it!" So we began to pray. We spent Wednesday nights praying. We began to study international missions and how it applies, what it means to be God's people on mission in Jeffersonville, Indiana, across the river from Louisville, Kentucky. We began to seek the Lord.

I remember the words of Harold, who was the eighty-eight-year-old chairman of the deacons. In this church, the deacon body led the church. Harold stood up one Wednesday night and pointed his finger at me and said, "Preacher, we'll do what it takes to reach this community."

We continued to pray and seek God and beg for his intervention for six months. During that season of prayer, God began to change us as a church body. We made radical changes in the life of the church, but the church made those decisions. They said, "Whatever it's going to take, we're going to reach this community."

The church decided that Easter would be the day for an intentional outreach effort. As Easter approached, people prepared the nursery, cleaned the balcony, and generally got to work. We had a church building that would seat about 250 people, and there were only 35 sitting down front (and a few who insisted on the back row).

Then Easter Sunday came—the day that had been set for the transition in worship time and style. Those thirty-five people had invited their kids, their grandkids, and even their great grandkids. They invited their neighbors and friends and prayed again. Two hundred eleven people came that Easter Sunday, and the church maintained an average of approximately one hundred in the weeks to follow. *What happened?*

The church grew over the next two years to an average attendance of just under two hundred. Today the church continues with multiple services. What happened was that their divot of the waffle moved, and they needed to figure out a new code. In 1952 this was a nice quiet suburban community that over time had transitioned, and their kids and their grandkids had departed. The church was struggling.

When they said, "We want to embrace the call of Jesus," the church moved to a new divot in the waffle. Their call was still to that neighborhood, that community. They began to reach out again, and the gospel began to take root. The church was changed, and their lives were transformed because of it.

Conclusion

It is not about us! It is about Jesus saying, "As the Father has sent Me, I am sending you" to "Go and make disciples of all different kinds of people" with a message of "repentance and forgiveness of sin" as a people who have "received the Holy Spirit." We are missionaries. Your church is intended to be God's missionary church. The only question is this: Are we being good missionaries? If we are going to be good missionaries, then we have to be willing to explore all of the divots in the waffle where he places or sends us.

We need to break the code on our "mission" field and find effective ways to reach the people to whom God has sent us. Breaking the code leads to breakthroughs—isn't that what all of us are seeking? The North American church, more particularly your church, must discern the strategies that will help you and your church break the missional code on your mission field. We must break through the cultural barriers in your community so that you can effectively reach out to all the peoples.

The Breaking the Code Challenge

1. In order to be sent what are some personal preferences you must overcome?
2. How can you help those you lead to see the divots in your community?
3. What does it mean for your church to be the missionary in your community?

Chapter 4

The Missional Church Shift

"The solution to health in a complex organic creature is to bring health to every cell of the body. If my church is spiritually healthy at its smallest unit—one disciple in relationship with one or two others with the DNA intact—and all of those units are healthy, we will have a spiritually healthy church. We view it from micro to macro."

Neil Cole

WHY DID GOD CREATE AND choose this institution called "church"? What is this gift that God has given us, and how does it impact our lives? *The church is one of the few organizations in the world that does not exist for the benefit of its members.* The church exists because God, in his infinite wisdom and infinite mercy, chose the church as his instrument to make known his manifold wisdom in the world.

Ephesians 3:10 tells us that God has chosen the church to make known his manifold wisdom. The church is the instrument and the vessel that God has chosen to use to reach your community. If the church is so central to God's redemptive purpose, then we should have a passionate desire to know how to make it more effective in its mission. However, wanting to reach people and growing a church to transform a community is usually not an easy task.

Nine years ago, my (Ed's) church growth world began to come apart.[1] Many of the surefire, guaranteed, great-new-whiz-bang programs weren't working in my church or the churches we were starting. They were supposed to work; they worked in other places, they worked for my friends, but they did not work for us! We kept trying them, but my community just did not respond as the experts promised. When I became a seminary professor, my students told me the same thing—the surefire methods were just not that surefire.

It took a while for us to figure it out, but the reality was that what worked in one place did not work with effectiveness everywhere else. The cultural code in my community (Erie, Pennsylvania) was different from the cultural code where the experts lived. We were living on different mission fields.

Today, we live on a mission field made up of all kinds of people—and they do not respond to the same approach. Blanket statements like "small groups are the only way," "Sunday school is the most effective method," or "you must have contemporary worship" are no longer appropriate (if they ever were). Instead, insightful pastors will seek to lead churches as missionaries. They will ask, "How can I take the unchanging faith 'delivered to the saints' (Jude 3) and present it effectively in a retirement community in Plantation, Florida, in an artists' commune in San Francisco, in a rural county seat town like Opp, Alabama, or on the Lower East Side of Manhattan?" By necessity, these churches look different because they are in different settings, but they also have one thing in common—they must engage their communities as missional churches.

As a church planter and pastor, I (Ed) experienced firsthand making the shift from using "canned" approaches to missional ones. While planting churches in the northeastern United States, we achieved success with certain methods and models. More than two hundred people came to the initial services of the last three churches we started. At first, direct mail provided a great tool to reach hundreds, but a few years later direct mail had less impact. A cultural shift was taking place that required a change in strategy and methodology.

We found that some methods worked elsewhere but not where we lived or among the people we were reaching. We learned that we needed a specific strategy to reach local people who were different from those in other parts of the country and world. The church growth movement had been beneficial, but it did not provide all of the answers. We needed to break the code in Erie, Pennsylvania, not in South Barrington, Illinois.

Church Growth

The church growth movement was started in the 1960s by Donald McGavran as a philosophy of foreign missions. Peter Wagner popularized the movement in the United States and Fuller Seminary in the 70s. The movement exploded on the evangelical scene in the 80s.

The church growth movement had its excesses and, rightfully in some cases, its critics. However, its fundamental question was, "How can we be more effective in reaching people?" Many are surprised to discover that before the church growth movement very little was written on how to organize a church for growth, welcome guests, or plan an outreach campaign. The church growth movement provided great new insights.

However, the church growth movement was too filled with methodological mania. Every book promised if you did what they said, your church would grow. Unfortunately, they told you to do different things. Soon, pastors were frustrated. They wondered to which guru they should listen, and soon, they decided not to listen to gurus anymore—they started listening to pastors.

Church Health

Despite all the good the church growth movement provided, its influence waned in the 1990s. Church leaders stopped looking to professors (most of the early writers were seminary professors) and started looking to successful pastors. They looked to pastors who had grown large churches. Soon, most pastors knew names like Rick Warren, Bill Hybels, and Steve Sjogren. They flocked to their churches for conferences. These megachurch pastors did not emphasize church growth but rather church health. They explained that healthy churches built around certain key values and a passion for the lost would grow.

Many pastors (us included) heard these insightful megachurch leaders and simply copied their methods. Soon pastors across the continent were wearing Hawaiian shirts, saying "lost people matter to God," and doing servant evangelism projects. Yet, many of the approaches used by these remarkable pastors did not work.

When they did work well, they usually were in similar communities. When Ron Sylvia planted Church at the Springs, he explained that he did it "by the book." In this case, he was talking about *The Purpose Driven Church* by Rick Warren. Lots of people have tried to grow a church similar to Saddleback, and it has worked in many cases. Ron is a highly gifted leader who had the insight to recognize that this approach would work in his church.

To be fair to our friend Rick Warren, *The Purpose Driven Church* is more of a description of Saddleback than it is a study of Warren's church health ideas. Those are more fully developed on his Web site, including a list of what does not make a healthy purpose driven church.[2] Warren explains that it has nothing to do with being contemporary, seeker-sensitive, etc. It is just that those methods, combined with some Willow Creek emphases, demonstrated a certain style (sometimes called "WillowBack") that many pastors tried to copy in their community . . . and it worked in some places and not in others. Ron exercised his spiritual giftedness and applied Warren's principles "by the book," and God blessed. (For Ron's story, check out his book *Planting Churches on Purpose*.)

So while many pastors have struggled with "doing church" in their contexts, successful pastors have discovered God's unique vision for their local churches, often learning from others. They became missional churches where God had placed them. They broke the missional code in their own neighborhoods instead of applying proven strategies of innovative pastors around the country, instead of focusing on church growth or church health gurus.

Church Growth → Church Health → Missional Church

The missional church is expressing itself in new ways. Pastors and church leaders are recognizing they are each on a unique mission field—right in their own neighborhoods. They are beginning to see themselves as catalysts for the advance of the kingdom—taking the unchanging message to their "changing context." This has led to several positive shifts in thinking. We will explore the shifts in the next chapter:

- from programs to processes,
- from demographics to discernment,
- from models to missions,
- from attractional to incarnational,
- from uniformity to diversity,
- from professional to passionate,
- from seating to sending,
- from decisions to disciples,
- from additional to exponential, and
- from monuments to movements.

The Missional Church

The church growth movement started as a missions movement. Donald McGavran was a missionary to India and learned his mission principles there. But, over time, and because of our burning desire to reach the lost, we sometimes focused too much on the programs, models, and plans and too little on missions. The church growth movement served the church in its time, and we should be grateful. But in this new millennium, we need a renewed emphasis on the church's missional beginning.

The missional church is not just another phase of church life but a full expression of *who* the church is and *what* it is called to be and do. The missional church builds upon the ideas of church growth and church health but brings the lessons learned from each into a full-blown missions focus—within their local mission field as well as the ends of the earth. To be missional means to move beyond our church preferences and make missional decisions locally as well as globally.

This chart may help illustrate the concept.

Church Growth	Church Health	Missional Church
Members as Inviters	Members as Ministers	Members as Missionaries
Conversion / Baptism	Discipleship	Missional Living
Strategic Planning	Development Programs	People Empowerment
Staff-Led	Team Leadership	Personal Mission
Reaching Prospects	Reaching Community	Transforming Community
Gathering	Training	Releasing
Addition	Internal Group Multiplication	Church Planting Multiplication
Uniformity	Diversity	Mosaic
Anthropocentric	Ecclesiocentric	Theocentric
Great Commission	Great Commandment	Missio Dei

Many leaders who call themselves missional focus on condemning church growth and church health. That is hardly a kingdom mentality. The reality is that each of these movements was blessed by

God to help the church care about reaching the lost (church growth) and become a holistic body (church health). The missional church builds on these things; it does not need to tear them down. Instead, a missiological, discerning application of the eternal principles from each movement can and does help the missional church.

The Sin of Preferences

One of the most important considerations in breaking the code is to break from our own preferences. Simply put, being missional does not mean doing things the way we like them. It means to take the gospel into the context where we have been called . . . and to some degree, to let the church take the best shape that it can in order to reach a specific culture. However, the problem is our preferences. You can't be missional and pick what *you* like at the same time.

We prefer some forms of music. We desire certain church organizational structures. We would like specific outreach plans. Simply put, we have certain things that we like. That is not a problem when our preferences line up with the missional choices for our community. The problem occurs when they do not. That situation requires a change of heart and the willingness to set aside our preferences.

That is not just an issue within churches (more on that below). It is often an issue with church leaders. Many times we think that the people within the church do not understand the culture. Sometimes they understand the culture better than we do! We often rush off to the next best conference of the month and come home and announce that this new model is the key to reaching our community. The people respond with, "That won't work here!" At that point, we assume that they are expressing a lack of faith. Often it just means that they have a better pulse on the community than we do. They think they know which kind of music, discipleship plan, outreach strategy, etc. will not work . . . and they are often correct.

On the other hand, churches are not always good barometers of the "outside" culture. Over time, a church culture develops that is separate from the broader culture, and soon it can no longer effectively understand the context around it. Churches become so tied to practicing their own preferences that they become the main goal, not the glorification of God within the culture where they are found. Rather, it is the glorification of God in a way that we find comforting and comfortable.

Many prefer not to worry about what people on the outside think, but just to take care of their needs and preferences.

> Before criticizing the escapist tendency of many
> Christians in America toward culture, we must
> confess that engaging culture is not an easy task.
> Engaging culture requires that we leave what is
> customary and comfortable, taking a journey of faith
> that we are not capable of making on our own. Engaging
> culture often means engaging with other cultures, entering
> into commitments—and even disputes—with those who
> have a different way of living. The very word *engage,* as we
> are used to hearing it, has connotations that often make us
> apprehensive, whether it's in the context of an approach-
> ing marriage or conflict with an enemy. Engagement is an
> act of commitment that could end badly, were it not for the
> faithfulness of God.[3]

Scripture teaches that we are to "consider others better than yourselves" (Phil. 2:3). This includes the truth that our preferences should never become more important than what our church needs to be and do missionally. For that matter, the church's focus should not be the preferences of other church members either. A truly biblical church will ask, "What will it take to transform this community by the power of the gospel?" not "How many hymns do we have to sing to make everybody happy?"

We find it intriguing to observe churches that are led by pastors with their own preferences (usually for the church to be more contemporary) who try to implement their preferences within existing churches (who have their own traditional preferences). They fight, they argue, people leave the church, and pastors even lose their jobs. The great fight of preferences could be resolved if only someone would ask the right question: "What kind of church would break the code in this context?"

The key to understanding the sin of preferences is to understand the need to overcome "preference slavery" and to become a slave to others. Paul is the model for us in that he made himself a slave to the preferences and culture of others, rather than a slave to his own preferences. The full context of 1 Corinthians 9:19–23 explains it better than simply stating "become all things to all men." It shows that it is about being a slave to the right things.

> Though I am free and belong to no man, I make myself a
> slave to everyone, to win as many as possible. To the Jews
> I became like a Jew, to win the Jews. To those under the
> law I became like one under the law (though I myself am
> not under the law), so as to win those under the law. To
> those not having the law I became like one not having the
> law (though I am not free from God's law but am under
> Christ's law), so as to win those not having the law. To the
> weak I became weak, to win the weak. I have become all
> things to all men so that by all possible means I might save
> some. I do all this for the sake of the gospel, that I may
> share in its blessings.

Churches that want to break the code must move beyond personal preferences into missional thinking. Or they must find a place where missional expression of church lines up with their personal preferences. The problem with finding a place to live out our preferences is that we are ministering on the basis of the very thing that will change: the culture around us.

Moving beyond preference requires a new motivation and outlook. More and more North American church leaders are finding the ability to move beyond preference in the tools of missiology.

A New Understanding

Missiology is birthed from our understanding of who Jesus is and what he sends us to do. Jesus said, "As the Father has sent me, I am sending you" (John 20:21). Who Christ is and how he is sent matters. How we do mission flows from our understanding of God's mission and directs our missiology. How we do church is grounded in Scripture but applied in culture. Thus, we have the intersection of who Jesus is and what has he sent us to do (Christology); the forms and strategies we use to most effectively expand the kingdom where we are sent (Missiology); and the expression of a New Testament church that is most appropriate in this context (Ecclesiology). All of these flow from and must be based on Scripture—and Scripture has much to say on each topic. For us to think we can make up new paradigms without consulting Scripture would be odd indeed.

Our thinking here is influenced by Frost and Hirsch's *The Shaping of Things to Come*, an excellent book seeking to apply missiological principles in a western context. Although we would see the process as more of an interaction than a progression, they challenged us to think missionally with a theological foundation of Christology, missiology, and ecclesiology. Van Rheenen's Missional Helix (http://missiology.org/mmr/mmr25.htm) helped us to see the process as an ongoing conversation and interaction of theological disciplines. Hence, the idea is a Missional Matrix: engaging all three theological disciplines in conversation and interaction. Alan Hirsch tells me he has moved in a similar direction himself.

The Missional Matrix must be birthed from Scripture. The Scripture presents some obvious teachings about who Christ is and about the mission that he gives us. Both of these are most clearly birthed from the Scriptures. However, ecclesiology and ministry are not simply a result of missional thinking. The Bible has much to say (and mandate) about church and ministry (see *Perimeters of Light: Biblical Boundaries for the Emerging Church*). Missiology impacts how these things are done, but the Bible requires that certain things should be done. Ecclesiology (and thus Church Growth) is not a blank slate to draw out of the cultural situation. The Bible tells us that certain things need to exist for a biblical church to exist. Certainly, *how* we do some of those things is determined by the context, but *that* we do them is determined by the Scriptures.

The following diagram entitled "The Missional Matrix" may help explain the interaction of Christology, missiology, and ecclesiology. The shaded circle illustrates the necessity of the scriptural and theological foundation and its Spirit-enabled application. Missional churches must begin and end with a solid foundation of rightly understood biblical theology. Only within this circle should Christology, ecclesioloy and missiology interact. Otherwise the church would be unbalanced and outside the bounds of Scripture.

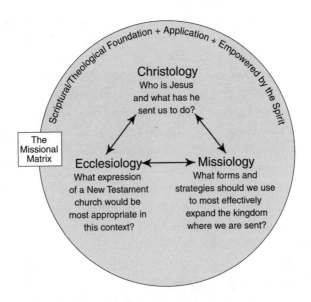

The church growth movement, most critics and friends would agree, sank into a church methods focus, many times without a foundation in scriptural truth. Thus, it strayed slightly outside of scriptural foundation and application. It touched on missiology, but often uncritically, without a proper understanding of anthropology, history, and mission-dependency issues. Finally, it was weakest in understanding the nature of the church as an extension of Christology. The result was an anthropocentric emphasis on tools and techniques, or methodology. This is illustrated in the following diagram.

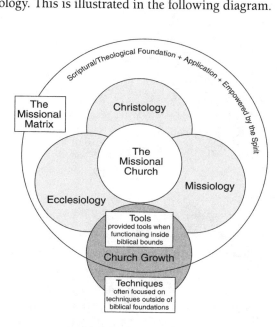

Rather than providing methods to grow a church, missional thinking helps the church leader to wrestle through who God has called him or her to reach. Missional leaders bring the gospel into a context by asking, "What cultural containers—church, worship style, small group ministry, evangelism methods and approaches, discipleship processes, etc.,—will be most effective in this context?"

Just as the church growth movement was man focused, the Church Health Movement was church/body focused. This movement centered on how the church body was related to Christ, and what was the best form of church (ecclesiology) in order for the church to be healthy. As mentioned before, this inward focus resulted in blindness to the community, blindness to other races, and blindness to other approaches. This approach is illustrated in the graphic of the following page.

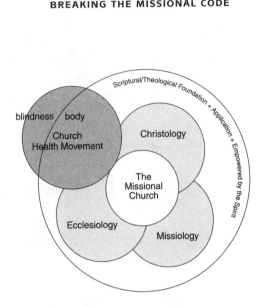

Of course, an emphasis on missiology and Christology without a proper emphasis on ecclesiology leads to a focus on being sent to the culture without an understanding of biblical foundations and biblical teaching about the church. When the church steps out of the scriptural and theological bounds in this situation, the result is syncretism—mixing up the gospel with the world so that you can't tell a difference.

George Barna's significant new book tells of more and more Christians leaving the church to find what they perceived to be a more authentic relationship with Jesus and others. Barna is not advocating everything that every revolutionary does, but he is reporting an important trend. He e-mailed us:

> Am I defining mere relationships as "church"? No. As you know, the Greek word *ekklesia*, from which we derive the English term church, is not clear to scholars but most of them agree that it generally has to do with the gathering of called-out people. So my notion of "being the church" requires that you be not only engaged in such passionate endeavors but that you also be connected to other believers

in some type of faith-oriented, regular meeting for the purposes of emulating and honoring Christ. Christianity is not an isolationist experience; it is covenantal and communal.[4]

What Barna is reporting has not yet been noticed by many in the evangelical church, but George Barna will heighten awareness with the publication of his recent book, *Revolution*. In one chart, he describes the transition to a Christianity less connected to the church but more in line with a spiritual syncretism that is taking place in our culture.

Primary Means of Spiritual Experience and Expression

	Local Church	Alternative Faith Based Community	Family	Media/ Arts/ Culture
2000	70%	5%	5%	20%
2025	30–35%	30–35%	5%	30–35%

Barna's purpose was not to critique the Revolutionaries but instead to report and even celebrate them. However, we think that those he describes show an undeveloped idea of what the church is— as described by the Scripture, not by the modern notion of church. These revolutionaries are often the children of the Anglo megachurch who are looking for something meaningful and authentic. Yet in the process of rejecting what we agree is in trouble (modern evangelicalism), if they fail to take God, Scripture, and church with them, they will become too tied to the world. In short, they become syncretized. (See graph on the next page.)

To navigate the changing of our culture, address the decline of the North American church, and provide for more theologically grounded practice, a new course is needed. We believe that this new course is a lot like the old one—a biblically grounded expression of

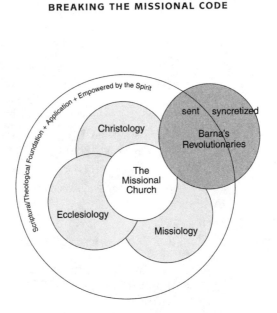

church that understands the person of Jesus, his call on their lives, what it means to be "on mission" in their context, and what it means to be an appropriate expression of church in their part of the globe.

The Breaking the Code Challenge

1. Review the chart on page 49. Circle one area on each row that best describes your church.
2. Based on your evaluation, where does your church fall? How would your church fit on the Missional Matrix?
3. What are some steps you can take to become more missional?

Chapter 5

Transitions to Missional Ministry

"I asked a lady, 'Would you come to church with me?' 'Oh, no, Ms. Tillie. Isn't church for people who have their lives together? I don't have my life together yet. When I get my life together, I'll come to church.' That's when I knew we must take church to the people. Our definition of church is what we do seven days a week, almost twenty-four hours a day, all year long! It is just who we are."

Tillie Burgin, Mission Arlington

CHANGE ALWAYS HAPPENS, AND MOST change is out of our control. What we can control is our response to a changing culture. The response by the missional congregation to change has produced emerging transitional patterns. As churches seek to break the code, they respond to change with intentional change. The changes involve transitions to a new missional focus.

The crux of the problem now facing North America is this:

In more homogeneous, traditional societies a message can be conveyed using concepts and language that are relevant to everybody. This is not the case in multiethnic and socially stratified urban societies impacted by modernity and postmodernity, where there is increasing differentiation and fragmentation. Society is splintered into a complex range of groups that collide with one another and reconfigure like the colored glass shapes in a kaleidoscope.[1]

Someone once asked Wayne Gretzky why he was a good hockey player. He answered that most players skate to where the puck is, but he skated to where the puck was going to be. The Bible refers to people like that: "Men of Issachar, who understood the times and knew what Israel should do" (1 Chron. 12:32).

We believe that the future will look a lot like today—only more so. Several shifts are beginning to take place in the lives and practices of missional churches. We have listed them as shifts because they represent a change of tone in the life of the church.

From Programs to Processes

As pastors, we remember waiting for the newest resources from the Fuller Institute of Church Growth. Every month new materials would arrive to help organize small groups better, lead people to give more, and show people how to bring their friends to a "Friend Day." Still, over time, we began to discover something strange: some of the best "stuff" did not work for us.

Books in the 1980s and 1990s explained that growing churches used telemarketing, revivals, direct mail, and Friend Days as their means of strategic outreach. But because not all of these worked for us, we found that the most important thing we could do was not to present the newest program or idea but to seek to understand the people we were called to reach and develop processes to reach them. Some of these tools were helpful but only tools *that would work among the people God had called us to reach.* (Unfortunately, very few writers said this—they usually said, "This is based on research, and if you do it, your church will grow." But they had not been to our community.)

For example, we have heard on many occasions the promise, "If you do this, X percent of the people will come to your church." Well, the reality is that we have both consulted and worked with hundreds of churches, and it seems to never work the same in two places. Instead, churches are recognizing that they need certain processes to help them accomplish their purposes. Those processes are universal, the purposes are universal, but the plan to accomplish them varies from place to place.

Church of the Apostles, an Anglican church in Raleigh, North Carolina, focuses their ministries on key areas and processes. They describe it as follows on their Web site:

Ministry teams are serving in these areas:

They utilize the metaphor of three streams and one river to describe their ministry focus. The three streams are represented by the following statements:

- The Church of the Apostles is built upon the clear teaching of the Bible.
- The Church of the Apostles celebrates the presence of the Holy Spirit in the body of Christ and not only welcomes the gifts that He gives, but seeks to minister according to the giftedness of the individual believers.
- The Church of the Apostles also celebrates two sacraments, Baptism and the Lord's Supper.

In addition to these three streams that make up one river, they organize their ministry around a number of teams designed to facilitate spiritual growth. They describe it as follows on their Web site:

Our ministry teams . . .

- Give us specific ways to serve Christ in our church and in our community;
- Provide opportunities for us to grow in Christ by serving;
- Allow us to grow in our relationships with each other by being part of a team who are serving together.

Ministry teams are serving in these areas:

- When we meet — teams who serve during our worship services.
- As we grow together — opportunities for growth for members and visitors.
- Children's Ministry — caring for children in a variety of ways.
- Student Ministry — serving the needs of middle school through college students.
- Missions — opportunities to serve both locally and abroad.[2]

A church that implements processes recognizes that the local congregation should function just like a human body (1 Cor. 12:12–20). Every part is influenced by every other part. The "body" of Christ is one unit that operates through a series of systems. Program orientation assumes the health of the overall system and does not see the various programs as interactive and interdependent. Therefore, it is destined to be ineffective. The only exceptions will be those churches with a process-focused approach or if the overall body of a church just "happens" to be healthy.

From Demographics to Discernment

Elmer Towns launched one of the most popular seminars ever in the 1980s. His "How to Reach the Baby Boomer" was one of the most influential seminars in the history of church growth. He was on to something—most Baby Boomers had similar values and could be reached by similar strategies.

Today, the generational approach does not work. The common characteristics of white, middle-class Baby Boomers are quaint memories in the new millennium. Some have tried to create the next "How to Reach the Baby Boomer," but it will not work. The growing diversity of our society is resistant to pigeonholing. Labels like GenX and Millennial have fallen into disfavor because they have lost their meaning. Demographics is not the answer. Instead, we need to decipher the individual communities to which God has sent us.

People are not asking, "How can I reach the typical GenXer?" Pastors are spending less time reading about the unchurched in North America as a way to find generic solutions to reach people in their context. *They are spending more time asking why the people in their community have not yet responded.* Like Jesus, they are spending time getting to know and evangelize lost people, not just looking for the next anointed style, program, or method. They are deciphering their communities and bringing the unchanging gospel to each community.

Kevin and Nancy Sullivan went to suburban Seattle to start High Pointe Community Church in 2000. Seattle is not a place where many evangelical churches thrive, so you would think that Kevin would be prepared to use the latest methods. Well, he did a great job preparing for the first service, but he did not just rely on the usual advertising tools. Kevin decided that a personal touch was needed to break through the barriers. He and his wife Nancy went door-to-door, five days a week, two to three hours a day, for several months, getting to know the community and introducing themselves to the people.

Over 450 people came to their first service. Today, over 1,300 attend in one of the most unchurched cities in North America. They found a way to break through the noise and connect with the people of Puyallup, Washington. The demographics would have said that door-to-door would not work, but Kevin had the discernment to see that the only way to reach this community was through personal contacts.

From Models to Missions

Every time we read a book from a church health pastor (particularly those mentioned earlier), he would warn—"Don't copy me. You are not in [my community]." We did not listen very well. As we look around us, we see that lots of other pastors did not listen very well either. As clones of successful megachurches popped up across the continent, the temptation was too great. We really wanted to reach as many people as they did, so we copied their models and hoped for the same results. Unfortunately, it did not work in most places.

Now, instead of importing styles and models, more pastors are genuinely asking the same questions that international missionaries do:

- What style of worship/music will best help this group to worship in spirit and truth?
- What evangelism methods should I use here to reach the most people without compromising the gospel?
- What structure of church would best connect with this community?
- How can *this* church be God's missionary to *this* community?

If we simply replace the church growth movement with a rush to copy innovative pastors, we will fail to engage effectively with the lost in our community. God did not call your church to reach Southern California, so it should not look like Saddleback or Mosaic. Instead, every church needs to ask what God is calling them to be and do.

Missiologists Michael Frost and Alan Hirsch explain in *The Shaping of Things to Come: Innovation and Mission for the Twenty-First Century Church* that Christology (our understanding of Christ) should shape our missiology (our understanding of his mission) and should shape our ecclesiology (our expression of church). Although some ecclesiology is specifically described in Scripture and is universally applicable, they are correct. The churches they are involved with in Australia reflect that.

They shared with me (Ed) that in Australia the idea of churches using "attractional" strategies to build bigger churches simply does not reflect sound missiology in their context. As they explained, the church in Australia has already reached all the people in Australia open to that model of church. Instead, they are creating smaller missional communities to reach their context.

From Attractional to Incarnational

In the eighties and nineties, church leaders were taught that the key to growing a church was to attract people with slick advertising, better programs, and good strategy. Those things are not necessarily bad, but leaders that break the code are recognizing that "nonrelational evangelism" is a contradiction. They are moving from attracting prospects to incarnating the gospel in their context.

Before we describe this, let us say that we are concerned about the overreaction by many pastors on this point. They have decided that anything other than one-on-one relationships is selling out the gospel. We do not agree. We think that is an overreaction, often based more on youthful idealism than good missiology.

In North America, "come and see" church outreach is still effective in many contexts but, usually, only when combined with relational approaches. In many places in North America, attractional is still missional, but it must be combined with incarnational ministry.

A church that is incarnational is interested more in the harvest than in the barn. For too long, the church has focused on getting the grain into the barn. We have made sure the barn is clean, made sure it is attractive, made sure it is well organized, and then, we assumed that the grains of wheat would make their way in if we invited them. Some did—but most people who could be reached that way already have been. Now, it is our job to move the church from solely attractional methods also to engage in missional ones.

Before going to Willow Creek, Randy Frazee pastored the Pantego Bible Church. He led the church to growth, not through the classic big service, but by challenging small groups to become incarnational expressions of Christ in their communities. They continue to do that by creating small groups geographically and expecting those in certain areas to attend certain small groups . . . and then for those small groups to transform their communities through presence, service, and proclamation. It will be interesting to see how Randy leads Willow Creek, perhaps the most famous attractional church, into a more incarnational expression of ministry.

From Uniformity to Diversity

If you wanted to grow your church fifteen years ago, you had to be seeker-sensitive. Other pastors might look down on you—you must not love the lost if you were not seeker-sensitive. Now, it seems that if you are not an emerging church, you must not be serious about reaching the lost. Fifty years ago, it was Sunday school. In the 70s it was bus ministry.

Today, people are realizing that God is using many different kinds of methods and models to reach different kinds of people. Yes, it is even O.K. to be traditional—as long as God is using your church to reach its community effectively.

To be fair, nobody thinks that their model is "a" model; they think it is "the" model. Reading about the emerging church is a good example. There is much criticism of Warren and Hybels and lots of angst directed toward the "modern church." That is interesting and thought provoking, but there must be a place for all kinds of biblically faithful churches. If churches are faithfully proclaiming the Word and reaching their communities, we should celebrate them, whatever they look like. The answer is not to make all of our churches look alike. The answer is to have everyone seeking the same thing: to glorify God by being an indigenous expression of church life where they are.

From Professional to Passionate

Ministry used to be the realm of the seminary-trained—not so anymore. Today, people (and churches) are looking for passionate and gifted leaders. Decades ago, professional training was the most important ingredient in becoming a successful pastor. Today, that is much less important to people in culture.

Some seminaries have recognized that their training needs to be more focused on the skills of spiritual leadership, and the quality of their graduates has increased dramatically. Theological education can and is helpful, but many leaders are seeing that they can be engaged in ministry without relocating to a school for several years.

Moreover, there is an increased interest in house church models. The point of the movement is that ordinary believers should be able to do the ordinary activity of planting and pastoring churches. Many will raise concerns, but how can we object to what was clearly the New Testament model?

Set Free Church is an example that we have mentioned earlier. The most important qualifications for leaders are God's call and a changed life. Those are the diploma requirements that have led Set Free to experience exponential growth.

From Seating to Sending

"Big" was almost always better in the age of church growth. In the age of the missional church, the impact of kingdom growth is more important. Church leaders who break the code have decided that the most important thing is to empower and release their church family for kingdom impact. These churches give themselves away rather than serve their own needs.

This is a big paradigm shift for most churches. For too long, we have spoken of "every member a minister," which was a positive step away from the professionalized ministry concept of the past. But for the church to truly break the code, it needs to move from "every member a minister" to "every member a missionary."

That means we need to change the "scorecard." Bob Roberts at Northwood Church is passionate about engaging his people in mission. I think a chapter in his new book describes it well. Bob asks, "What do you get when a church combines Billy Graham with Mother Teresa?" The answer is Northwood Church—reaching out and transforming its community for Christ.

That is why both of us are deeply committed to church planting as a preferred ministry approach. Both of us have church planting Web sites to help planters (David's is www.churchplanters.com and

Ed's is www.newchurches.com). For us, the size of our churches is less important than the transformation of community, nation, and world through church multiplication—not just people gathered, but people sent.

From Decisions to Disciples

Probably the most important recognition of the last thirty years is that our statistics do not line up with our reality. For too many churches, we supposedly win thousands to Christ every year, and yet few follow through and become active disciples.

Many people have criticized the church for being too shallow over the last twenty years. They were right. However, often those who made this criticism were in churches with fine teaching and in-depth discipleship, yet they were reaching very few people.

I (Ed) still remember a well-known preacher lecturing a group of pastors about their need for more focused preaching and discipleship. He told them that they needed to be more sober, more serious, and train their people. Once the people were filled with the Word and well taught, they would become witnesses. So I did what I probably should not have done—I called and checked on how his church was doing in evangelism. This well-known church was filed with well-taught people, but very few people were coming to faith in Christ and being baptized. It is easy to criticize; it is hard to achieve both decisions and disciples.

Probably one of the more common questions is, "Should churches focus on better disciples or focus on reaching out?" The reality is that we need both. You cannot have one without the other. You cannot separate evangelism and discipleship. We need missional churches that are focused on serious disciple making, not just leading people to make a decision. For this to occur, we must identify what a disciple is (see chapter 9 on spiritual formation). As we fully define a disciple to include both the inner disciplines of personal spirituality and the outer disciplines of missional living, then we will move our churches to be filled with missionary disciples like the early church.

From Additional to Exponential

As the evangelical church matures, it is beginning to understand that all healthy things reproduce. One of the signs that something is "living" is that it reproduces. There will certainly be a place for large megachurches that break the code, but they (and other missional churches) know that it is more than just addition; it is exponential multiplication that matters.

We have all heard the vision for multiplication. Someone gets up, draws on the white board, and explains that 2 x 2 x 2 x 2 soon reaches everyone in the world. But let's face it, *there is not much addition going on, let alone multiplication.* Yet some churches are realizing that giving themselves away for multiplication is better than just constantly trying to gain a few additions.

When I (Ed) planted Millcreek Community Church in Erie, Pennsylvania, our church was one of only a few of our denomination in that area and the only one that was strong. We decided to grow by multiplication as well as addition. We planted two daughter churches on our third anniversary. Many of the people in our church did not understand why, when we were averaging only 350 and were only three years old, we needed to send out fifty to seventy-five of our people to plant two new churches in one day. We made the decision because we believed that there would be more people in the kingdom through the power of multiplication.

What we believed has proven true. Millcreek is larger, but New Hope and Lake Pointe are also reaching their communities. They, in turn, have helped plant four other churches. Hundreds more now worship Christ than would have if we had just grown Millcreek by addition.

Several years and one thousand miles later, the church that I (Ed) am planting now (Lake Ridge Church) thinks that waiting three years is a sure sign of a lack of faith. We have asked the Lord to help us be "born pregnant." Our plan is to start our first daughter church within a year of starting worship—and at least one church each year after that. We have already set aside 20 percent of our budget for mission in our church—before we have had our first service.

This is not the easiest way to begin a church. It takes sacrifice to set aside that much of your limited funds when you are only a launch team. But this is where faith has to overcome human logic. Churches always seem to "put off" their participation in church planting until they are "larger." This is true of churches of one hundred and churches of one thousand. There is never a "good" time to send money, people, and energy somewhere else. Nevertheless, it is the only true way to engage in God's work of exponential expansion of his kingdom.

From Monuments to Movements

There have been few true people movements to Christ and his church in North America. Perhaps there were movements of God during the awakenings, but they were soon stifled. It seems that our culture tends to turn movements into monuments before they spread too far.

Pastors tend to build monuments to themselves and monuments to their churches. It seems that every pastor really wants to get into mission—if his church was just a little bigger. They do not want to give themselves away until there is enough to share. That is not the way God does things. God calls us to give ourselves away and trust him.

Earlier, we mentioned Bob Roberts. Both of us consider Bob a friend. He has made choices that challenge us. For example, while he could be leading one of the largest churches in Texas, he has decided to plant ten new churches a year. He sends out rather than keeps. God has blessed the church (they are building a two-thousand-seat auditorium right now), but his focus is on exponential growth, not just addition. Tens of thousands of people in his daughter churches are glad that has been his focus. He has been striving to promote a movement of God, not to build a monument to himself or his church.

These shifts are both helpful and challenging. They challenge the church and leaders to be apostolic. By "apostolic," we are not speaking of the authority, power, or oversight of the first-century apostles. That office has passed away. However, the meaning of the a word *apostolic* is best defined as one who is "authoritatively sent." We are sent to proclaim the gospel from Christ, who, before giving the Great Commission, began by reminding his listeners, "All authority in heaven and on earth has been give to me. Therefore go . . . ." Jesus authoritatively sends us to proclaim the gospel and reach people in the name of Christ, not to lord it over in new structures of church life. Some claim "apostolic" focus on *their* authority, but our focus is on *Christ's* authoritative commands to go and transform the world for the gospel—in our church, community, and culture.

Thus, these shifts are forcing the church to focus more sharply on its apostolic mandate. We are rediscovering that to be a biblical church means to be missionally engaged . . . and those shifts help us to think biblically and missionally in our world.

The Breaking the Code Challenge

1. Identify specific areas listed in this chapter where you need to transition to a more missional approach.
2. Describe how these specific areas need to be transformed in your specific context.
3. What would your church look like if it was truly missional?

Chapter 6

Values of Leaders and Churches That Break the Code

*"We don't care if you're wearing a suit or a T-shirt and jeans.
What we care about is the condition of the heart."*

Gary Davis, Church in the Wind

BREAKING THE CODE IS NOT about programs; it is about values.
Code-breaking leaders think differently, and this results in churches
that make a difference. For each leader and their churches, breaking the code includes spiritual formation, discipleship, reaching the
unchurched/unreached, evangelism, culturally relevant expressions
of church, and spiritual warfare.

Values of leaders and churches that break the code spring from
the firm knowledge that following Jesus is a way of life that trans-
forms us to be the incarnation of Christ in every culture.

The good news is Jesus transcends all cultures. Jesus is not modern. Jesus is not postmodern. And his body, the church, is neither modern nor postmodern, though it lives within both cultural paradigms. Ultimately, Christ's community is a way of life that incarnates into and challenges any and every culture, in every time, in every place. Mission is an intrinsically translational task. Throughout history, God has shown himself relating to people within their cultural frame of reference. The life and work of Jesus Christ set a pattern for the church's mission. In the incarnation, God became more than words. The Word himself entered culture in a specific time and space (John 1:14).[1]

That formation into a community, a way of life, enables and empowers us. That spiritual formation makes it possible to be the church God calls us to be.

Spiritual Formation

Those who break the code are committed to their own spiritual formation. While working with the North American Mission Board we conducted an exercise with about three hundred mission strategists around North America. We asked them to identify the barriers that decrease our ability to impact culture through rapid church growth and multiplication in North America. They came up with over five hundred different barriers. After doing an initial analysis, we concluded that 71 percent of their responses related to issues of the head and heart.

As we observe effective leaders around the globe, there is no doubt that their effectiveness is the result of their capacity to create a culture that addresses head and heart issues. This is always reflected in their own spiritual formation. There are at least six areas that intermesh with leadership effectiveness. They are the leader's calling, character, competency, comprehension, commitment, and courage.

Calling

Leaders who break the code have a strong sense of calling. This calling is often characterized by a specific place and/or people. Leaders who look for opportunities seldom break the code. Leaders who break the code create opportunities. Former NFL coach Mike Ditka described leaders as those who either "find a way or make a way." They are motivated by the need and a sense of calling to a certain people or place. They throw themselves at the challenge of creating environments where the gospel can be planted and flourish.

Character

Leaders who break the code lead out of a high sense of moral authority. Leadership becomes an issue of influence, not position. This kind of influence in a healthy environment only flows out of character—when a leader's words and actions are aligned. When people observe this kind of character over the long haul, they become willing to invest themselves in the leader's vision and dreams.

Competency

For the most part, leaders who break the code figure it out for themselves. That does not mean they are unwilling to learn from others. On the contrary, they study widely what others have done. However, these leaders recognize that every context has its own unique challenges. Breaking the code happens through trial and error. As a leader takes risks and either succeeds or fails, he learns from each situation and uses that information to plan for the future. Each experience helps build a new level of confidence and competence.

Comprehension

While competence is built over time through experience, comprehension is the result of a commitment to learning all one can from others. While many leaders are intuitive in their approach, most leaders advance because they are committed to the discipline of their profession or calling. We have observed that the most successful church planters make a point of reading everything on the subject—because it is the passion of their life. Successful pastors often report a mentoring relationship filled with learning conversations. Many great leaders describe how they have visited other great leaders from around the globe prior to engaging in their venture. Leaders do whatever it takes to learn and prepare for success and significance.

Commitment

Breaking the code doesn't happen without commitment. Perhaps this is the greatest challenge for leaders. How do we pay the price without bankrupting our lives and ministries? However, there is no escaping the reality that breaking the code is hard work and requires an incredible amount of commitment.

Courage

Perhaps one of the most underestimated areas in breaking the code is courage. Leaders who break the code have a high level of courage in regard to making the tough decisions. They are almost rude about vision. They have the courage to protect the unity of the church. They hire and fire the right people. They are simply willing to make the tough calls to break through.

Discipleship

Those who break the code are committed to making and multiplying disciples. Many pastors have learned the hard way that you can attract a crowd and still not have a church. You can build a church and not make or multiply disciples. Those who break the code are incredibly committed about making disciples. They may not be the best disciplers, but they are committed to developing processes, raising up leaders, and building organizational structures that produce true disciples.

My (Ed's) own church experience here stands as a painful lesson. The church we planted in Pennsylvania grew rapidly in numbers but not in maturity. We found that our intentional outreach strategy worked, but we had no effective strategy for making disciples. We spent a painful second year fixing our mistakes and moving forward to develop a new strategy that would make disciples.

Earlier we mentioned Set Free Church in Yucaipa, California. They have obviously broken the code among urban bikers. Their discipleship process involves a number of strategies. They conduct outreach events at public parks or other places where their ministry focus group congregates. They give a concert, preach the gospel, give people a hotdog and drink, invite them to accept Christ, and go to the ranch. At the ranch, these converts dry out and begin an intense Bible study routine. From there, they begin attending the church, get involved in learning a trade, and become meaningful members of their community and church. Others attend a one-year Bible school and are sent out to start other outreaches, ranches, and churches.

Making and multiplying disciples involves three things: (1) living like Jesus lived, (2) loving liked Jesus loved, and (3) leaving behind what Jesus left behind. Therefore, breaking the code involves understanding what it means to make and multiply disciples and then being able to apply it to one's context. Making disciples among urban bikers in Southern California looks radically different from making disciples among urban professionals just a few miles away in Orange County. However, it all begins with a commitment and understanding of what it means to make and multiply disciples. This includes living like Jesus lived.

Live Like Jesus Lived

When Jesus called his early followers, he called them into a way of life that was radically different from the one they knew. What began with a simple invitation, "Come, follow me" (Mark 1:17), became an incredible command. He gave the disciples two things to help them follow him—power and a picture. He could have simply given them power, but he spent nearly three years modeling the life that he intended for them to live.

Many people have rejected the church because of those who claim to be followers of Christ. It is painful but true, "The world isn't interested in Christianity because we Christians aren't known as people who live what we say."[2] Until we move beyond superficial faith, we will not experience supernatural living.

As a disciple, we too are to model life as Jesus did. We are to invite people to come follow us as we follow him. Philippians 2:5–8 describes how Jesus approached his own existence. We often refer to this as the "downward spiral."

> Your attitude should be the same as that of Christ Jesus. Who, being in very nature God, did not consider equality with God something to be grasped, but made himself nothing, taking the very nature of a servant, being made in human likeness. And being found in appearance as a man, he humbled himself and became obedient to death—even death on a cross!

Most of these breakthrough pastors took the downward spiral. In some cases, instead of pastoring existing churches, they chose to take a risk and start a new church. They chose not to rely on what was already in place but sought to start something new—even though it may have cost them financially and was harder work. In other cases, they did the hard work of turning a church around—a risky and dangerous proposition.

Living like Jesus lived is a downward spiral. While God may not call all of us to sell everything and go to Madrid, Spain, he calls all of us to "deny ourselves and come follow him." Amazing things happen when we teach people to live like Jesus lived.

Love Like Jesus Loved

Living like Jesus lived is one thing; loving like Jesus loved is another. Story after story in the Gospels reveals how Jesus loved. Obviously, it is the very core of what his character is all about. Jesus teaches us that this love is far more then a feeling, but it is a commitment that is lived out in our behavior. It is a radically different language than we are used to speaking.

Most of us believe that love is something we feel; it is related to those who make us feel good. Jesus taught us that it is a commitment we must have toward all people, regardless of their relationship to us. Teaching people to love like Jesus loved begins by modeling this love to them. Love is passed on as they see us demonstrate it in all kinds of environments and situations, in spite of our circumstances. Jesus taught and demonstrated this kind of love everywhere he went in the context of doing community with his disciples.

Leave Behind What Jesus Left Behind

What did Jesus leave behind? He left people who lived like him and loved like him. Those who break the code are not only committed to making disciples; they are committed to multiplying disciples.

Neil Cole is an excellent example of a follower of Jesus who is committed to leave what Jesus left behind. He has been closely associated with the house or organic church movement in the United States. He heads up Church Multiplication Associates (CMA) that "exists to facilitate church multiplication movements by focusing resources on reproducing disciples, leaders, ministries and churches."[3] Here is what Neil had to say in a recent annual report:

> I want to be honest with the facts. While it appears by the numbers that we are multiplying, upon more careful examination I find that our growth is mostly addition rather than multiplication. A few of our networks are forming with new converts and reproducing, but many are forming churches from Christians who lost their passion for the

kingdom and have now been re-ignited with our vision and form of spiritual community. This is not a bad thing, but we must not be content until we see the lost found and the communities we live in transformed by the powerful presence of the kingdom of God. Keep your eye on the ball!

I would say we have done well at reproducing disciples and even churches, but we have not yet begun to see the reproduction of leaders, networks or movements. We have added leaders and networks to our family but not yet multiplied them. With that in mind our commitment this next year is to focus on what it takes to reproduce CMA itself. Pray with us as we pursue this calling.[4]

It is obvious that Neil and his organization are committed to leaving what Jesus left behind.

Reaching the Unchurched/Unreached

Those who break the code are committed to reaching the unchurched/unreached. Both of us grew up in non-Christian homes. I (David) experienced Christ for the first time in a significant way when my father became a Christian. Prior to that he struggled with alcoholism, and the chaos in our lives reflected that. You can describe the transformation in his life as a radical transformation. Everything about our lives changed.

Two years after he became a Christian, my father sensed a calling and became the pastor of his first church. His ministry was not only characterized by the life change we experienced as a family but also by the life change we saw everywhere. For years, we saw people come to faith in Christ every week. As a new Christian, with no other frame of reference, I thought this was normal. That is, until I left the church he led to serve in other churches.

The more I moved away from my father's ministry, the more I saw a huge divide between those on the outside of the church and those on the inside. Everyone talked about evangelism, but few did evangelism. The contrast between the words and the actions was radical. To talk about reaching unchurched/unreached people is popular. To actually develop a church that sees its mission clearly, creates an environment for reaching the lost, and implements an effective strategy that wins people to Christ is a much greater challenge.

Churches that are breaking the code are paying a high price for reaching the unchurched/unreached. They are discovering that churches that focus on the unchurched/unreached often create a degree of discomfort among some churched/reached. In other words, you cannot have it both ways—either the lost like you or the satisfied religious crowd likes you.

We have pastored and been around many churches that have made a commitment to focus on the unchurched/unreached. In churches that move to Christian maturity, satisfied churched people often miss the point. Instead, they want to go "deeper" with "meat." Ironically that "deep meat" is often a focus on the obscure or unclear in Scripture rather than on the life-changing nature of what is clear.

The irony is that most people crying for "meat" are really crying for minutia. They want to learn the deeper truths about the times of the rapture rather than how to live the Christian life. True meat teaches people how to be transformed by the renewing of their minds so that they will live like Christ, love like Christ, and leave what Jesus left behind. But believers in church-focused ministries often think that it is more important to teach about controversial subjects rather than transformational truths.

People who want life-transformational preaching and teaching will find such at churches that break the code. Furthermore, they can and do go deeper—through deeper biblical study in the church but also through their own study.

The chart below describes four potential ministry focus groups. They are the churched/reached, churched/unreached, unchurched/reached, and the unchurched/unreached. While any church will have all four areas represented, those who break the code are committed to reaching the unchurched/unreached and moving them to Christian maturity.

We are not opposed to or do not lack appreciation for churched/reached individuals, but if their experience has been a more traditional or program-based type of church, they are more than likely going to want more choices when it comes to programming and teaching. That does not mean that they cannot be a part of your ministry, but it does require an intentional strategy to help them make the transition and come to understand that, at least in this case, less is more.

CHURCHED/ REACHED	CHURCHED/ UNREACHED
UNCHURCHED/ REACHED	UNCHURCHED/ UNREACHED

In this context, there are four questions that those who break the code ask either intuitively or overtly. They are: (1) Where are the unchurched/unreached? (2) Who are the unchurched/unreached? (3) Why are they unchurched/unreached? (4) What is God already doing among the unchurched/unreached?

Where are the unchurched/unreached?

This question relates to places. Supposedly, in some places in North America the culture is more Christian than in other places. On the other hand, in many communities there are no Christian churches, or the population is so massive that the few churches that exist in that area are insignificant. In other places, there are churches, often many churches, yet none of the churches speak the language of the people who live there.

Who are the unchurched/unreached?

This question builds off of "place" but goes a step further by asking who these people are in this particular place. This question takes into consideration population and population trends, housing and housing trends, and household trends. Are the unchurched in this place white singles age twenty-one to thirty-five, living in urban upscale high rises and who moved here because of the many service jobs that cater to the affluent? Are the unchurched in this context young couples who are moving to this suburban context because of the family values and the professional jobs on the north side of the city, make $75,000 to $100,000 every year, and live in $350,000 houses? Obviously, both of these groups need to be reached, but the methods of breaking the code will look very different with regard to each one.

Why are they unchurched/unreached?

In *How To Reach Secular People,* George Hunter describes four barriers that unchurched/unreached people have to cross in order to become Christians. The *image barrier* relates to how people view Christianity. This question addresses barriers related to why people are unchurched/unreached. It assumes that for many they have not found a church that is relevant to their life. They view the church as boring, irrelevant, arrogant, and sometimes simply untrue. If we are going to develop relevant churches, it is important to identify through our research specific barriers and issues that answer this question of "why" a certain people group, population, or those within a certain cultural environment as a whole are unchurched. For them, attending a church can be as intimidating, sobering, and irrelevant as it would be for many of us evangelicals to walk into a bar or club on Saturday morning at 1:00 a.m.

The second barrier is the cultural barrier. Hunter refers to this barrier as the "stained-glass barrier" and goes on to add: "When secular people do visit a church, it can be a culturally alienating experience. If they do not understand the jargon, relate to the music, identify with the people, or feel comfortable in a facility, they infer that Christianity (and the Christian God) is not for people like them."[5]

A third barrier Hunter identifies is the *gospel barrier*. He adds that this is the only legitimate barrier unchurched/unreached people should have to face. The gospel is a barrier that requires regeneration and repentance as well as a radical new direction. The last barrier he mentions is the *total commitment barrier*. Once a person crosses the gospel barrier, there is a call to total commitment.[6]

The point that Hunter makes, and we want to reinforce, is that we should do everything we can to remove all image and cultural barriers. The more effective we are at removing these types of barriers, the more effective we will be at reaching the unchurched/unreached. This idea of specific barriers will be developed further in a subsequent chapter on spiritual formation.

What is God doing among the unchurched/unreached?

It is arrogant to assume that God is not already at work in most places. We need to ask, What is God doing? Where is he blessing? As we discover what he is doing, we must learn from others and join God in how he is already at work. Those who break the code join God in his activities.

Evangelism

Those who break the code are committed to culturally relevant expressions of evangelism. In a recent conversation with Reggie McNeal, author of *The Present Future: Six Tough Questions for the Church,* we were discussing the reason that our denomination's church-planting efforts plateau at a certain point. I (David) suggested to him that the reason was related to maxing out our financial system. We simply could not afford to plant more churches. He quickly disagreed, suggesting that the real reason was that we had reached everyone like us or everyone who wanted to be like us. He explains it this way:

> In North America the invitation to become a Christian has become largely an invitation to convert to the church. The assumption is that anyone serious about being a Christian will order their lives around the church, shift their life and work rhythms around the church schedule, channel their charitable giving through the church, and serve in some church ministry; in other words, serve the church and become a fervent marketer to bring others into the church to do the same. In my denominational tradition, I grew up with a euphemism used to describe when people became Christians: They "joined the church." The reduction of Christianity to club membership can't be said better than that.[7]

What we are discovering is that those who are effective in breaking the code understand that there has been a radical shift in how we do evangelism. We can no longer just appeal to people to come "back" to an institution of which they do not remember being a part. With this fading memory, proclamation evangelism has decreased in its effectiveness. Asking people to literally change their worldview after simply hearing the gospel, with no previous exposure to a Christian worldview, is usually unrealistic. While churches that effectively evangelize the unchurched/unreached do not abandon proclamation evangelism, they set it in the context of community, experience, and service.

Community

The gospel has and always will continue to travel best along relational lines. What we have discovered is that where churches are exploding with life change, the people are connecting with the message of the gospel through relationships. It is not unusual for the most effective evangelists to need evangelizing themselves. Like the woman at the well who brings her entire village to meet Jesus, entire households and neighborhoods are showing up at these churches that break the code.

If the late twentieth century experienced individual conversion, the early twenty-first century has swung the pendulum back, and we are once again seeing entire households being evangelized, similar to the New Testament model. In a recent conversation, a pastor told me (David) that forty-two families out of his subdivision were attending the church he pastored. Knowing the church, I understood that most of these people are coming because he planted the gospel among them, and through relationship after relationship, the gospel has flourished. Churches that break the code focus on building environments in both large and small groups, both on and off the campus, where the gospel can thrive.

Experience

In addition to community, experience plays a key role in churches that break the code. Obviously, you cannot have community and not have experience. Churches that break the code put a high premium on experience. This usually involves the environment they create and the prayers they pray. By inviting the unchurched/unreached into community in both large and small groups, we are inviting them to experience the life that takes place within the Christian community. Because they often have no reference point for Christianity, this is important.

No longer can we distinguish between the mission field and North America. In a missional context, individuals often begin the discipling process long before conversion. This takes place as they actively experience community and participate in the ministries of churches that are breaking the code. They see the drama of redemption played out before them, and they become active participants in this drama.

Service

At Mountain Lake Church, we are in the process of discovering the power of volunteerism. Almost overnight our young church has exploded from four hundred to nearly two thousand in average Sunday attendance. Most are coming from the unchurched/unreached pool. The question becomes, How do you assimilate hundreds of new people into your church each year? The answer is, We do not know! But we are putting them to work as volunteers, and we are moving them into small groups. In putting them to work through volunteerism, we are seeing many of their lives changed. While there are places where you only want believers and church members to serve, there are many places you can plug in those who are on the journey. We have found that when people are involved in ministry, something happens that speeds up the process of their spiritual journey. There is something about being "affirmed and accepted for who I am" that opens a person's spirit to consider deeper spiritual issues.

Culturally Relevant Expressions of Church

Those who break the code are committed to culturally relevant expressions of church. Harvie Conn suggests that "people must be able to say, 'God speaks my language.' In the churches where that occurs, growth may often be fast and sure."[8] When we develop churches that speak the language of their community and at the same time hold true to the changeless truth of Scripture and the gospel, we become successful at breaking the code. Our churches become truly indigenous to their context, and the gospel is able to flow unhindered by cultural barriers.

Although in many areas this type of contextualization needs to take place, churches that break the code pay close attention to this kind of cultural relevance in the way that the message is communicated, worship is experienced, disciples are made, and evangelism takes place. In these churches, each of these areas is unique and either very intentionally or intuitively given a significant amount of attention. These specific areas will be discussed in detail in the next chapter.

Spiritual Warfare as Spiritual Formation

Before moving to that discussion, there is one other area that code-breaking churches value—spiritual warfare. Any time we speak of spiritual issues and the life and ministry of the church, we have to consider spiritual warfare. Unfortunately, many books on spiritual warfare are just, well, odd. There is talk of mapping strongholds, conversing with demons, and almost a demon in every doorknob. However, if we miss this important principle because some have taken it too far, we will not break the code in our community. A church's spiritual formation must include spiritual warfare.

We find some odd things in the Bible about spiritual warfare. Spirits seem to be assigned to territories, demonic forces tend to resist and retard the growth of the kingdom, and the lost and unchurched are spiritually blinded by Satan. It may seem odd in our modern era, but part of breaking the code is to become aware of all the factors that hinder the work of God in a community—and then to address them head-on.

For us, that involves seeing the strongholds that Satan already has in a community. The first church that I (Ed) planted, was in Buffalo, New York. I soon discovered strongholds of apathy and false religion that held back the growth of the kingdom in Buffalo. I was in the inner city, so we also saw many other obvious strongholds. Today, we serve in north Georgia, one of those places where young professionals flock to get away from the problems they associate with the city. Here, strongholds of consumerism and image are everywhere.

To break the code, we need to recognize and pray against the cultural and spiritual strongholds of our communities. How? Well, when we pray for people, we pray that God will do his work in their hearts and break down strongholds of disobedience, and we pray for the Holy Spirit to do his work.

The process of breaking strongholds is not unlike the process of exegeting a community. Both of them require an understanding of the community, its history, and its people. By observing the people and the culture, we understand both who they are and what strongholds are at work. We will discuss that in further detail later.

Conclusion

In summary, churches that break the code do not do it by accident. No one can deny the presence and power of God in a church that experiences favor with him and their community. All of these churches are relentless in their love and devotion to Christ. They are eager to give God the glory. Often, they struggle with talking about themselves. Yet at the same time, God has chosen to work through them to bring glory to himself. Breaking the code is a discipline of seeing your context through missional lenses and then exercising faith by taking the necessary risks to live the Great Commandment in such a way that you can fulfill the Great Commission.

The Breaking the Code Challenge

1. Identify the values that you must have if you are going to break the code.
2. Which of these values challenge you the most?
3. How can you put these values into action?

Chapter 7

Contextualization: Making the Code Part of Your Strategy

"We're unlearning the amount of anonymity and space desired by our guests. Lost people usually want connection and answers or they wouldn't be showing up. They find it very compelling when they authentically connect with God in worship, especially when we involve all their senses."

Ron Martioa, Westwind Community Church

CONTEXTUALIZATION OF THE GOSPEL IS needed in every culture, but it seems to be in particular need in the West today. British missiologist Stuart Murray-Williams explains the pressing reasons for the need:

- Recognition of a yawning cultural chasm between church and contemporary culture that hinders movement in either direction. Church members struggle to bridge the gap at work or relaxing with friends; many know their friends will find church incomprehensible, irrelevant, [or] archaic.

- Inherited forms of church are attractive only to certain subcultures (especially white, middle-class, educated and middle-aged conformists) and are ineffective in mission beyond these.
- Alarm that we are losing from our churches many former members who are not losing their faith but find church uninspiring, disempowering, crushing and dehumanizing. In post-Christendom, institutional loyalty and inertia no longer prevents this hoemorrhage of disillusioned Christians.[1]

Obviously the gap is widening when it comes to the distance our culture feels from the church today. Quickly, those of us with a Christian worldview are becoming the minority. This is changing even in the Bible Belt—known for being culturally adaptive to Christianity. More and more churches are finding that their neighborhoods and subdivisions are made up of people who struggle with a Christian worldview or a positive predisposition of the church.

According to *The Christian Index,* a newsletter published by Georgia Baptists—the largest religious group in the state—the number of people who are outside the church is rising at an alarming rate. "While a string of annual reports have shown an increasing number of baptisms, a rise in church membership, and growth in attendance in worship and Sunday school, those figures offer a false sense of security when viewed against a background of real population growth. While more Georgians are finding faith in Christ, statistics indicate that nearly 70 percent of the state's 8,383,915 residents remain unchurched."

If this is so, then it is important that we ask the question how we can reintroduce people to church and ultimately to Christ. Here are some important observations that we see played out in the life of churches that continue to break the code.

- In today's context the average person finds the church through the personal invitation of a friend or coworker who has typically previously been unchurched.
- The majority of people inviting others to attend a weekend service are still disconnected from Christ and have only

recently started attending weekend services or exploring and experimenting with the faith themselves. Sometimes they experiment and explore with several different faith options.

- Those who attend who are formerly disconnected from Christ and the church often attend for several years before going public with an expression of faith in Christ.

- Those who attend often participate in many aspects of church life prior to going public with their faith.

- Those who go public with their faith often have been discipled and grounded in the faith long before going public. Conversion, in this context, becomes part of the discipleship process.

- Those who are formerly disconnected from the church who find Christ and assimilate into the church seldom fall out of the church. Change seems to be lasting.

This is not necessarily the kind of church that many of us are most familiar with—which leads us to a discussion on "how do we present the gospel and church in a culturally relevant way without compromising the truth?" For years, overseas missionaries have wrestled with this and similar questions. They have built successful missional strategies on concepts like indigenization and contextualization; this leads us to a discussion on how to apply a code-breaking strategy within a local context.

This will not be without its risks (or failures), but the faith is about biblically informed risks. "Peter was not a failure because he looked down and began to sink. If anyone failed, it was the eleven who stayed in the boat, waiting to see if it could be done."[2] Too many churches are afraid to take risks to reach their community . . . until it is too late. Instead, they need to become intentionally indigenous.

Indigenization

The idea behind indigenization is that a church should spring forth out of the soil in which it is planted. It is indigenous in that its leadership, expressions, forms, and functions reflect that of the context. At the same time, it serves as a transforming agent in the very culture that sustains it. When this happens, we can truly say we have an indigenous church.

What we have found is that when the pastoral leadership, core of the church, and community all line up, the potential for the church to take on an indigenous form is significant. This combination seems to provide a greenhouse for explosive growth. The chart below illustrates the relationships that we are talking about.

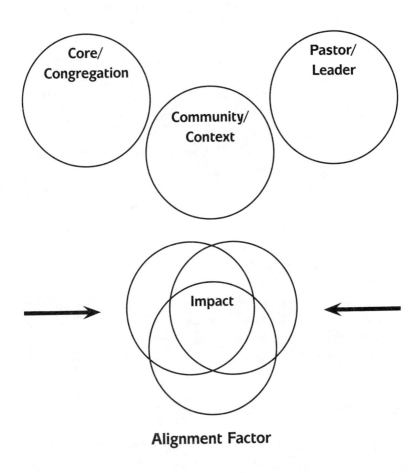

Alignment Factor

The churches mentioned throughout this book and *Planting Missional Churches,* even though very different in terms of form and style, are good examples of indigenous churches.

A common mistake that many churches make is to do a nation-wide search for the most talented leaders. However, if the leadership does not emerge or fit the context, it is our observation that the impact is short-lived or limited, regardless of the leader's talent level. In many of these churches, leadership most often comes out of the community. They seldom hire outside of the community. Musicians come from their community and leaders come from their community. Their style reflects their community, communication reflects their community, and resources come from their community. As a result, person by person, their communities are being transformed.

Contextualization

If the church is to become an indigenous expression of its context, then contextualization comes into play. When it comes to contextualization, reality suggests that the eternal, universal truth of God's Word is understood and appropriated by people through a cultural grid or framework. It is vital to note that though we understand and appropriate the truth as conditioned by culture, the truth itself should never be compromised. On the other hand, many previous cultural adaptations within the church over time can become part of our tradition. Over time, these traditions can become the barriers that we must remove if the gospel is to be incarnated among other cultural groups.

The Way the Message Is Communicated

Starting Point

By far the most controversial point of this whole discussion is the way the message is communicated. Many in the Christian church suggest that the only way to communicate the gospel is through verse-by-verse expository preaching. Others like Rick Warren have adopted what he calls a topical exposition approach. Still others like Dan Kimball, in *The Emerging Church,* talk about a theotopical approach. The issue here is not whether you approach Scripture from an expository perspective or a topical one; it has more to do with your starting point.

Most Christians prefer to begin at the point of biblical revelation—"Thus saith the Word of God!" For us, a simple reference to John 3 or Psalm 32 means that we are about to hear something important and relevant to our lives. From biblical revelation, we move toward application or relevance. Based on what God's Word says, here is how we need to apply it to our lives. For those who are disconnected from Christ and the church or even new believers, their beginning point can be very different. They are often ignorant regarding any expression of Scripture and, at the very least, neutral toward it if not hostile.

As one person in our church asked: "How many books do you Christians use? I hear you talking about the Old Testament and the New Testament. The other day it was the book of John and then it was the book of Luke. How many books do you use?" This is not uncommon in our culture today. For those with no biblical reference point, the beginning point is often that of relevance. They are asking, "Does this have anything to do with my life?" Or "Is it relevant?"

Paul demonstrated this when he was invited to speak to a completely Jewish audience after entering a synagogue in Pisdian Antioch; he began with the Old Testament. While he did not quote directly from the Old Testament, he began by summarizing its historical account. "Men of Israel and you Gentiles who worship God, listen to me! The God of the people of Israel chose our fathers; he made the people prosper during their stay in Egypt, with mighty power he led them out of that country, he endured their conduct for about forty years in the desert, he overthrew seven nations in Canaan and gave their land to his people as their inheritance. All this took about 450 years" (Acts 13:16–20).

On the other hand, when Paul was in front of a very different audience in Athens, his starting point was different. We read in Acts 17, "Paul then stood up in the meeting of the Areopagus and said: 'Men of Athens! I see that in every way you are very religious. For as I walked around and looked carefully at your objects of worship, I even found an altar with this inscription: TO AN UNKNOWN GOD. Now what you worship as something unknown I am going to proclaim to you'" (Acts 17:22–23). The apostle Paul began where the people he was speaking to were. For the Jews, the starting point was their ancient history rooted in the Old Testament Scriptures. On the other hand, Paul connected with the Greeks at their point of relevance. Notice that he presented Christ in both cases. For us, we may start in a different place, but the context of the message needs to be Christ and the fullness of Scripture. The key is where the communication begins. Scripture sets the agenda and shape of the message, but every message needs the question, "Why is this important to me/us?" If there is no point of connection, the message is simply meaningless facts rather than life-changing truth.

Redemptive Analogies

When we begin at the point of relevance, it does not in any way nullify the importance of rightly dividing the Word of God. We think that a common mistake many seeker-driven churches made early on was trying to communicate relevant messages that had little or no biblical content. It seemed that the sermons were basically explanations of common-sense wisdom, or perhaps biblical principles, but the Bible did not set the shape or agenda of the message.

We must always remember that "consequently, faith comes from hearing the message, and the message is heard through the word of Christ" (Rom. 10:17) and "the word of God is living and active. Sharper than any double-edged sword, it penetrates even to dividing soul and spirit, joints and marrow; it judges the thoughts and attitudes of the heart" (Heb. 4:12). The Bible is not simply a tool for scriptural footnoting or common-sense wisdom.

One of the cultural shifts that we are experiencing is the shift from the secular to the spiritual. This shift lends itself to biblical preaching and teaching. People are looking for a higher power, a sense of mystery, revelation, and spiritual authority for their lives. Scripture was given to reveal Jesus; therefore, all of our preaching should be Christ-centered. With this in mind, we must ask, "How do we communicate the good news of the gospel in a way that the story of redemption is heard and experienced?"

In our highly spiritual world, we must look for cultural bridges that we can cross in order to carry the good news to a spiritually hungry people. Don Richardson gives us great insight regarding this in his books *Peace Child* and *Eternity in Their Hearts*. Using the concept of redemptive analogy, he describes the importance of finding a common cultural understanding as a tool for sharing the gospel with the Sawi or other people groups. In an interview by Dick Staub, Don gives the following account of this concept:

> When Caroline and I lived among the Sawi and learned their language, we found that they honored treachery as a virtue. This came to light when I told them the story of Judas betraying Jesus to death after three years of friendship. They acclaimed Judas as the hero of the story. It seemed as if it would not be easy for such people to understand God's redemption in Jesus. But lo and behold, their way of making peace required a father in one of two warring villages to make an incredible sacrifice. He had to be willing to give one of his children as a peace child to his enemies. Caroline and I saw this happen, and we saw the peace that resulted from a man's wonderful sacrifice of his own son. That enabled me to proclaim Jesus as the greatest peace child given by the greatest father. In *Lords of the Earth*, the Yali tribe had places of refuge. That was their special redemptive analogy. In other words, there's something that serves as a cultural compass to point men and

women toward Jesus, something that is in their own background, part of their own culture.[3]

In breaking the code, we must look for those cultural bridges to every people group, population segment, and cultural environment. Obviously, this may look very different from one group to another: As I was preaching recently, I (David) told the story of how I searched for and gave my wife a diamond ring for our twenty-fifth wedding anniversary. I related this to Luke 7, the story of how Mary poured expensive perfume upon the feet of Jesus. My point was to illustrate how impractical God's expressions of love can be. I related it to the cross and how, "While we were still sinners, Christ died for us." My goal was to build a cultural bridge by using a story to which people could relate. I wanted them to see how impractical God's love for us is and at the same time, how impractical his love through us should be toward others.

Redemptive analogies are twenty-first-century parables. They are like the stories Jesus told. They are examples and stories that bring truth about the kingdom of God to life in the common language, stories, and symbols of the day. They are like the trilogy that Jesus spoke of in Luke 15, where he talked about "lostness" by using the example of a lost coin, a lost sheep, and a lost son. All three of these analogies related to the culture of his day, and the common person could place himself into the reality of any of these stories. The stories illustrate the demonstrable love the Father has for us.

Experience

Dan Kimball reminds us of the shift from knowledge-based communication to experience-based communication in *The Emerging Church*. Even though Kimball is primarily concerned with emerging cultures in his study of people groups, population segments, and cultural environments, we find that many of these groups have more similarities with emerging cultures than a modern culture. It appears that modernity is slowly on its way out. With this in mind, it makes sense to pay attention to what the emerging church is learning. Kimball drives this point home by quoting *Leadership Network*:

> *The shift from knowledge to experience.* Experience is the new currency of culture. In the past we gained knowledge of subject or issue and then later validated that knowledge. Today, people have an experience that is later validated by knowledge. . . . This shift has implications in the way we learn, communicate and interact. For churches it impacts the design of worship, liturgy and the shape of and content of educational ministries, the process of spiritual formation, the design of sacred space, and programming.[4]

On the facing page you will find an invaluable chart that Kimball calls "Shifting Values in Approach to Preaching" explaining the contrast between communication approaches and the importance of experience in many of today's contexts.

Now, it is important to note that this chart is not designed to advocate one approach over another, but it is directed toward those who are communicating to emerging culture. Many places and population segments tend to be much more modern than postmodern. However, as we move away from modernity, for whatever the reason, we have to recognize that there is a difference in how we approach communication.

Nor is this to say that in emerging cultures one size fits all. This is exactly our point in breaking the code—many cultures exist in North America, and if we are to be effective at planting the gospel among these different peoples, we must learn to communicate the gospel in a way that is more missional than pastoral.

Modern Church	Emerging Church
The sermon is the focal point of the worship service.	The sermon is one part of the experience of the worship gathering.
The preacher serves as a dispenser of biblical truths to help solve personal problems in modern life.	The preacher teaches how the ancient wisdom of Scripture applies to kingdom living as a disciple of Jesus.
Emphasizes the explanation of what truth is.	Emphasizes the explanation and experience of who truth is.
The starting point is with the Judeo-Christian worldview (Acts 17:1–3).	The starting point is the Garden of Eden and the retelling of the story of creation and the origins of man and sin (Acts 17:22–34).
Biblical terms like gospel and Armageddon don't need definition.	Biblical terms like *gospel* and *Armageddon* need to be explained anew.
The scriptural message is communicated primarily with words.	The Scripture message is communicated through a mix of words, visuals, art, silence, testimony, and story.
Preaching in a worship service is the primary way one learns from the Scriptures during the week.	Preaching in a worship gathering is a motivator to encourage people to learn from Scriptures throughout the week.
Preaching takes place within the church building during a worship service.	A lot of preaching takes place outside the church building in the context of community and relationships.[5]

The Way Worship Is Experienced

This leads us to a discussion on worship. When speaking about worship, we are referring to the practice of worship in the context of community. It is important to note that worship must take on an expression that reflects the culture of the worshiper if it is to be authentic and make an impact. Numerous "worship wars" are going on in the local church in North America today. The reality is that *most of these battles are based on traditions and personal preferences, not biblical authority.*

When it comes to worship, a good starting point is to determine the purpose of worship. The seeker churches in the eighties and nineties pioneered the seeker-targeted approach to worship. Their focus was on nonbelievers to the extent that many did not call their weekend services "worship." Churches like Willowcreek offered alternative "worship" services during the midweek for believers. They functioned based upon the premise that you could not do church for seekers and believers together.

At the same time, there were many churches that had failed to see the huge shift in our North American culture and did church as if everyone had a positive predisposition toward Christ and the church and were firmly grounded in a Judeo-Christian worldview. As we know, this simply was not the case, and these churches became known as believer-targeted churches among many church growth leaders and students. A third group that emerged is often referred to as the seeker-sensitive church. These churches worshiped in a way that focused on believers, but at the same time, they sought to make their worship seeker comprehensible.

The challenge with two of these approaches related to the tension that exists between seeker-targeted worship and believer-targeted worship. The degree to which a worship service is seeker-targeted is in direct proportion to the degree to which it is believer-hostile. The same is true in that the degree to which a worship service is believer-targeted is in direct proportion to the degree to which it is seeker-hostile. The following graphic illustrates this relationship.

When it comes to seeker-sensitive worship, this tension is acknowledged, but there is also recognition that it requires other seekers and believers coming together in order for worship to be everything that God intends it to be. In the New Testament several things emerge as it relates to worship:

1. Worship was for believers (John 4:23).
2. Worship included both believers and seekers (1 Cor. 14).
3. Worship was to be expressed in such a way that it did not become a stumbling block to seekers (1 Cor. 14).
4. There were times when worship was conducted in a public forum where large groups of nonbelievers were engaged (Acts 2–3). With this in mind, many churches see the purpose of their worship gatherings as a place and time where they can create a safe environment for both believers and seekers to experience life change. This happens when the worship gathering takes on a form and expression that is familiar to the cultural group.

Churches that break the codes recognize this and are served by asking questions like these:

1. Is the setting inviting and familiar?
2. Are those attending and participating familiar with the music?
3. Can those attending and participating relate to the communication style of the preacher/teacher?
4. Is the Bible being taught in a way that people can experience and grasp the message?
5. Is the language used understandable and true to biblical content?

6. Is the way in which people are invited to participate in truth clear and engaging?
7. Is the environment safe for those in process?
8. Is there enough tension created to cause people to move forward in faith?
9. Does the creativity used connect with those attending and participating?
10. Is Jesus clearly lifted up in the worship experience? Is worship God-centered?
11. Is the gospel clearly presented?
12. Are people given a clear opportunity to respond?
13. Are they invited to participate in community on a regular basis?

The Way Evangelism Takes Place

Once again the challenge related to evangelism in today's context is determining the starting point. In most cases, we are not simply asking people to say yes to some propositional truth with which they already agree, but we are talking about leading people to change their worldview. A primary aspect of this reality is the time required for worldview conversion and the context in which that takes place. It would be similar to asking the common person in Columbus's day to accept his theory that the world was round after that person had always assumend that it was flat. Therefore, evangelism should be less programmatic and more process-oriented. At the same time, it should be less propositional and more relational.

I (David) recently received a phone call from a major evangelism group wanting to interview me concerning our evangelism programs and methods. I am not sure why they called our church or how they knew of our existence. At the same time, however, we believe that we are learning many new things related to evangelism and that we are having a significant impact in the area of adult conversions and baptisms. We recently reviewed our denomination's annual church report. Even though we seldom if ever turn in a report, we gained some perspective when we realized that we were in the top one hundred churches out of forty-three thousand when it comes to number of people baptized. I say this because I want you to know that, even though our approaches are different from most organized church evangelism programs, the value and expression of life change is at the top of the list of who we are. We are totally committed to reaching out to disconnected people. I believe that is true for many churches that are breaking the cultural code.

In the interview, I was asked a number of questions like "What evangelism program do you use?" "How do you train your people to do evangelism?" "How could we serve your needs for evangelistic training?" A few years back in a different context, I could have answered all of these questions with some kind of affirmative answer, but my response was, "We don't have any of these things, and I don't know that you can help us right now." As a matter of fact, we have resisted any formal types of evangelism training. We have spoken very little in public about direct evangelism. We seldom if ever do any kind of servant evangelism. We have done some, and we talk about it on occasion. But we always go back to "if it's not broken, don't fix it."

Having said that, we have landed in another world, and it is no longer flat. The observations that we made earlier in the chapter hold true in regard to what we are discovering about evangelism in many contexts. The focus has changed. People are no longer starting their spiritual journey near the cross or even facing the cross. The way we engage people in a meaningful way is radically different. It is a shift to journey.

This assumes some very important things, such as:

- Trusting God to be at work in the lives of lost people.
- Building relationships with all kinds of people and valuing who they are.
- Listening and learning where God is already at work in their lives.
- Praying that God will reveal to you and give you words to share with others on their journey.

- Helping them connect the dots between their story and Jesus' story.
- Being a third testament by becoming a "living epistle."[6]

Regardless, if these are the exact premises our context calls for in breaking the code, it becomes obvious that we must rethink our approaches to evangelism. It is important to note that, while we have spent time singling out evangelism, it is one part of a larger process that involves the entire disciple-making process and should never be seen as a solitary component.

Simply put, evangelism needs to be returned to an ecclesiological (church) focus—the focus of evangelism is people coming to faith in Christ through God's chosen missional instrument, the church. Conversion is part of discipleship. As God works in the lives of men and women, they have already begun their spiritual journey, and conversion is one step, albeit the most important one of all.

The Way We Make Disciples

A number of years ago, we began to observe an interesting trend in many of our new churches that attracted a large number of unreached/unchurched people. It seemed that the longer individuals took to finally go public with their faith, the less likely they were to fall through the cracks or go out the back door. On the other hand, when someone came in and rather quickly expressed a commitment to Christ, they seemed to disappear just as quickly.

Recently, in an interview a missionary returning from Malaysia was asked about his personal evangelism approach. He noted this in the culture from which he had just returned, when someone experienced conversion, they were already firmly grounded in Scripture, often engaged in community, and usually involved in some kind of service within the church. Discipleship in this context began long before conversion, and conversion was simply part of the discipleship process. North America, like Malaysia, is now a mission field, and many of the realities of an international mission field are equally valid here.

Later in this book, we will discuss the discipleship process and give a model that includes: searching, believing, belonging, becoming, and serving as part of the discipleship process. However, it is important to understand the following principles as they relate to discipleship:

1. Discipleship begins prior to conversion. It is important to note that more and more in today's context conversion will be part of the journey and will often require years of participation in a local congregation before a person goes public with his or her faith. Churches that break the code will be required to figure out how to do church in such a way that facilitates this journey.

2. Discipleship involves participation in community prior to conversion. Churches that facilitate this journey will recognize the importance of relationships, the currency that moves the unreached/unchurched forward. As believers recognize that they are missionaries, they will find more and more ways of engaging those outside the church in authentic relationships. Small group ministries will more and more reflect the culture of worship gatherings that are inviting to large numbers of unreached/unchurched people. Churches that recognize this will need to spend more time figuring out how to connect the unreached/unchurched with their small group ministry.

3. Discipleship often involves participation and experience prior to conversion. Churches that understand the discipleship process are also proactive about creating strategic and specific experiences for those who are on the journey. Each step toward the cross is celebrated as a victory. Worship gatherings are designed to create space where people can experience God and progress at their own pace. Unreached/unchurched people are invited to participate and experience God on a variety of levels, first

as observers, then as participants in worship.

4. Discipleship often involves participation in service prior to conversion. Churches that break the code recognize that God uses people to accomplish his purposes. Sometimes these people are mature disciples; other times they are in the early part of the journey. When one outside of faith is used in a simple way, they are affirmed and most often move forward in the journey. These code-breaking churches recognize this and create all kinds of opportunities for the unreached/unchurched to participate in service.

5. Discipleship often involves participation in missions prior to conversion. In a recent mission meeting, a lady stood up and said: "I know God is working in my life. He has answered my prayers and healed my husband of cancer. I don't understand him and haven't made up my mind entirely about him, but I'm on a journey. So I'm going. My next step is to go to South Africa and provide humanitarian help with my church." It is these kinds of experiences that become most meaningful to many people who are on the journey.

In addition to recognizing that conversion is only part of the disciple-making process, it is important to note that churches that break the code are serious about conversion and make a big deal about people going public with their faith, and they recognize the importance of continuing spiritual growth.

A common misunderstanding related to some emerging and missional churches is that they downplay conversion because they facilitate conversion differently. This is not true. In most cases, there is a stronger emphasis on conversion and celebration of those who are going public with their faith.

When it comes to continuing discipleship beyond conversion, churches that break the code often use more organic means of discipleship, but just as intentional. Ongoing discipleship often involves small groups, one-on-one mentoring, and service with others outside of one's comfort zone. What it does consist of is as important as what it does not consist of—a feed-me-more-meat mentality.

Churches that grasp these mission concepts and understandings often see significant results in terms of impact. In addition to contextualizing communication styles, worship expressions, evangelistic processes, and discipleship processes, there are numerous other areas that need to be considered. Many of these areas are obvious, and once a commitment is made to break the code, opportunities are endless.

Contextualizing the Church

1. Based on the definition of *indigenous* on pages 91–92, what does it mean for you to be an indigenous church?
2. Evaluate how effective you are at contextualizing the gospel in the areas of communication, worship, evangelism, and discipleship.
3. What are some practical steps you can make to become more contextually relevant?

Chapter 8

Emerging Strategies

"Our problem was that people were showing up and the town shut down any expansion hopes. We aren't content whenever people are going to hell if we can make a difference. . . . At first we thought the resistance was the devil, but actually expanding to multiple campuses was the best thing we could do—God had his hands in it."

Byron Davis (Lay Leader), Seacoast Church

INNOVATION IS A GOOD THING. When churches seek new ways to reach their communities, it means they are open to seeing God at work in fresh new ways. These new expressions demonstrate an increasing desire to reach people. Interest in church planting seems to be increasing significantly. Churches are now seeking to reach new areas through multisite venues. The megachurch is not declining as many predicted. It is becoming the norm in many settings. Finally, more house churches and other incarnational expressions are on the increase. All of these issues come with challenges and dangers, but they are appearing because the North American church is beginning to point in a missional direction. More and more evangelicals are seeking ways to impact the lostness of our culture in a way that has not occurred in North America for some time.

Church Planting

In 2004, I (Ed) did a survey for the North American Mission Board. We identified and contacted 124 organizations, denominations, churches, and agencies. They were asked several key questions including, but not limited to, the following:

- Has interest in church planting increased or decreased in your sphere of influence in the last ten years?
- Describe your church planting systems including recruitment, training, and multiplication.
- How do you recruit and involve sponsor churches?

The final article based on this research can be found in the *Journal of Evangelism and Missions* and was published originally there. The most noteworthy finding was that not one respondent indicated a decreased interest in church planting. In fact, all but two of the groups indicated an increased interest, and none indicated a decline in such. Moreover, many indicated that their interest in planting churches had increased dramatically.

This increased interest may also be reflected in the number of books published on the subject of church planting. From 1996 to 2002, there were only two mainstream books published on the subject. As a seminary professor teaching church planting in 1998, I struggled to find adequate textbooks on the subject. However, from 2003 through 2005, at least eight mainstream books have been published on the subject, and many others are forthcoming. Evangelical churches have rediscovered church planting. The interest is so significant that we have dedicated a chapter to that subject in this book.

Multiple Venues for Mission

A few years ago, the idea of "one church, two locations" sounded strange. Today, it is a common strategy. As churches have sought to break the code in their contexts, they have considered multiple expressions, locations, or venues as a key to their strategy.

Multiple expressions. This entire book has been about the importance of the people being able to experience church in a language they understand. We must continue to encourage, support, allow, and experiment with new expressions of the same biblical church in new cultures. Breaking the code will continue to require that we open our eyes and see the many harvests. In reality, the harvest looks radically different than it did just a few short years ago. If we are to fulfill the Great Commission, it may require us to have many expressions of church often on the same campus, certainly in most geographical contexts.

Multiple services. A few years ago churches had multiple services out of necessity. We know that typically when your seating is at 80 percent capacity you are at your space limit. One solution was to add a service. We can still remember the days, not too long ago, when many churches preferred to build a larger worship space. That is simply not an option or preference today. I (David) recently stood in the new worship center of one of our large megachurches. It seated eight thousand people. As you examine the emerging megachurches around North America, they are simply not going in this direction. Churches of all sizes are choosing to have multiple services for many reasons. Multiple services allow churches to:
1. maintain intimacy and community even while experiencing rapid growth,
2. provide multiple worship time options,
3. provide services designed for specific people groups or population segments, and
4. continue to free up the high response service times for disconnected people.

In short, churches are choosing to offer multiple services for strategic purposes.

Multiple locations. In addition to multiple services, many churches are beginning to use multiple locations as a strategy for fulfilling the Great Commission. In a report from Leadership Network, *multiple-site/multiple-campus churches* and a number of other multiple location approaches are highlighted. They seem to be represented by three basic approaches: multiple-site/one teaching pastor, multiple-sites/multiple teaching pastors, and multiple-sites/video venues. According to Dave Travis, the driving forces behind this movement include starting multiple-sites/multiple-campuses for the following strategic reasons:

- as a church planting strategy,
- when targeting a new age group (usually younger) or a different psychographic group,
- when it is impossible to expand existing facilities,
- to establish a new worshiping congregation based on the worship style/format,
- as a special purpose "branch" such as an institutional setting, prison, nursing home, etc.,
- to reach a new language or ethnicity different from the original congregation, and
- to "help" a fellow church of the same denomination.[1]

Dave has identified some common challenges related to this approach that must be answered in order to develop this type of code-breaking strategy:

- What is the role of the preaching/teaching team?
- What is the role of the campus pastor?
- What is the role of music/drama/arts leadership for each congregation?
- How do you maintain the staff's focus?
- Which staff and volunteers are critical to start another site?[2]

Warren Bird notes in a Leadership Network article, "Extending Your Church to More Than One Place: A Field Report on the

Emerging Multi-Site Movement," that there are "at least 1,000 churches across North America (that) could be described as multi-site." He goes on to note that Elmer Towns has been observing this trend for a number of years; he wrote about it in his 1990 book, *Ten of Today's Most Innovative Churches*. Three of those ten churches have modeled what Towns calls "one church meeting in many locations . . . a multi-staffed church, meeting in multi-locations, offering multi-ministries, with a single identity, single organization, single purpose, (and) single force of leadership."[3]

House or Koinos Church

There is a tremendous increase in interest in house churches among evangelicals. Some of the higher profile church planting networks only plant house churches. Mike Steele, North American director of DAWN Ministry, a prominent mission ministry, told us that he can identify 150 networks of house churches across North America.[4]

Though the term "house church" is very acceptable in the movement, some use other terms. We prefer the term *koinos,* a Greek word that is used infrequently but emphasizes an "all thing in common" approach to church. Koinos churches function in completely relational manner, whether they meet in a home, clubhouse, or coffee shop.

In recent years, much has been written regarding the subject of churches that function without buildings. Since the most recent emphasis on house churches began in the late 1990s, much of the literature appears on the Internet. Because of the growing interest in house churches, it might be helpful to answer the question, "What is a house church?"

First, a home cell is part of a larger church and supports the ministry of that church. Most churches planted in the last few years have a large celebration service for worship accompanied by meetings in homes for small group care. On the other hand, a house church is different in that it is not part of a larger church; *it* is a church.

Second, koinos churches do not start in a home and then move to a larger, rented, or permanent facility. The house church is different. As it grows, it will *multiply,* not *enlarge.* The home is their permanent facility; it will remain a koinos church—always connected by face-to-face relationships.

It is difficult to define the house church because it has so many expressions (and some are cults, sects, or just filled with strange people). The ones making an impact are not fringe groups or sects, but instead, these groups represent New Testament Christians seeking to be faithful in becoming a biblical expression of God's church in their local context. Unfortunately, many have experienced the "sect" groups and think that all house churches belong in the same category. In many cases, that is an unfair stereotype.

Finally, one other word is helpful to the person unfamiliar with the house church movement. Koinos churches often exist in networks; they are not isolated, independent groups of Christians. They are related to other house churches in a regional area. These koinos churches often meet together for fellowship with other house churches, but it is not usually on a weekly basis. In addition, these network meetings are not seen as "real church." Real church takes place every time a particular koinos church meets.

If a house church is genuinely a *church,* then it should function as one. The Bible teaches that churches have pastor/elders and other leaders. Biblical churches covenant with one another. Churches participate in the Lord's Supper and baptism. All the characteristics of a New Testament church need to be present in a house church for it to be a biblical church.

In the New Testament, "the word 'church' was applied to a group of believers at any level, ranging from a small group meeting in a private home all the way to the group of all true believers in the universal church."[5] Many biblical passages refer to local house churches (1 Thess. 1:1, the church of the Thessalonians; Rev. 2:1, church at Ephesus, etc.). However, part of the challenge is that many enthusiastic house church proponents have neglected some of the ecclesiology described in Scripture by deemphasizing New Testament delegated leadership, misunderstanding the role of covenant and related church discipline, and failure to practice the biblically prescribed ordinances:

Church is well described as

> an autonomous local congregation of baptized believers, associated by covenant in the faith and fellowship of the gospel; observing the two ordinances of Christ, governed by His laws, exercising the gifts, rights, and privileges invested in them by His Word, and seeking to extend the gospel to the ends of the earth.[6]

Part of the challenge is confusion about the fact that "two and three" can "gather" in his name, and Jesus "is there" (Matt. 18:20). The presence of Christ does not necessarily mean that a local church exists in that context. A church, as described in Scripture, has certain elements that make it a *church*.

The increased interest in koinos churches is a sign that evangelicals are open to new missional approaches. That is good news. However, as with any new emphasis (or in this case a reemphasis of New Testament practice), evangelicals do not need to just search the Scriptures for permission to function in the manner described. We also need guidance in how to implement the practice—taking into account the full biblical teaching on ecclesiology. Biblical house churches can and are another missional approach for kingdom impact.

Some Interesting Developments Around the World

While this book is primarily about the church in North America, there is much we can learn from the church around the world. Frankly, many of those churches look more like our future churches than those that exist in North America today. While some of these expressions of church greatly challenge those of us who are most familiar with a churched culture, it is important that we take time to acknowledge and learn from them. In an occasional paper, *The*

Realities of the Changing Expression of the Church, produced for the Lausanne Committee for World Evangelism, a report of fifteen unique expressions of churches from around the world was presented. While we are familiar with many of these expressions of church, three stand out as unique. Like most missional churches they are way out on the fringe of what is happening and warrant a closer look.

Marzahn Youth Church in East Berlin, Germany

A team of seven full-time and five volunteer youth workers and church planters set off in the fall of 2000 to plant a church among the youth in East Berlin. This section of Germany is "thoroughly and emphatically atheistic." According to their leadership, "Looking around Berlin, especially the eastern part, it is a fact that church growth among adults is exceedingly slow. . . . For this and other obvious reasons, such as the fact that youth are in the midst of transitions and much more open to new ideas than adults, we deliberately decided to focus on young people. We are not unaware of the problems and challenges associated with a youth church. . . . We view the youth church as a bridge into the community, as a beachhead or an arrow which can penetrate the hardened souls and hearts of a post-communist mentality."

They go on to state in breaking-the-code fashion, "The question we are asking ourselves is: 'What must happen so those youth of East Berlin, who are still greatly influenced by their parents' atheistic philosophy, can become believers?' Here is an attempt to answer that question:

- They must hear the gospel in their culture.
- They need the examples of changed lives.
- They need the loving and inviting communities of the body of believers.
- They need to experience God.
- Their old atheistic and materialistic worldview must die."

At the time this paper was being written, they had seen twenty young people make commitment to Christ and forty to fifty attend a weekly celebration with a vision of a church of two hundred by the year 2007. While the work is slow, it is extremely encouraging."[7]

A House Church Among Japanese Nurses

Rethinking Authentic Christianity (RAC) was relaunched in 2002 with a vision for planting house churches in Japan. That group found success planting house churches in "homes, school campuses, and Starbucks coffee shops." During this time, one increasingly open population segment of Japanese culture was nurses. This group exhibits three interesting characteristics:

1. They want to be healed. Due to the stress of always serving others and being constantly surrounded by the sick and dying, they are tired and in need of both emotional and spiritual healing.

2. Many are involved in the New Age movement. They know the limitations of medical science. Some of them care for those who are dying and/or suffer from hopeless conditions. So the nurses tend to search for spiritual answers to questions about our finite human existence.

3. They give serious thought to the well-being of life. They are scientific people and are good at analyzing their psychological problems. But they have not been able to find the answers to the pressing questions in their lives. They are seriously seeking hope, purpose, happiness, and acceptance.

RAC recognizes that breaking the code did not come without its challenges and required addressing a number of theological issues:

- Headship of Christ in the midst of a family-like small group.
- Priesthood of all believers.
- Meeting the felt need of seeking spiritual power.
- Supernatural intervention can be found in Scripture.
- Taking back the power of imagination from the enemy.
- Judge the fruit in each case.
- Every spirit should be tested.

Again, it is important to note that RAC had to address each of these theological issues in a culturally relevant yet biblical and authentic way. Finding this kind of balance is part of the challenge of breaking the code.[8]

Factory Mission in Hong Kong

In addition to these three examples of emerging types of churches, George Hunter gives another excellent example. Dr. Agnes Liu of Hong Kong's China Graduate School of Theology and "her colleagues observed that Christianity in Hong Kong was a middle-class movement, that working-class people were essentially unreached. The project began with extensive research of working-class culture; Dr. Liu worked months as a seamstress in a factory to learn working-class culture, dialect, vocabulary, values, needs, heroes, and heroines. She became intimately familiar with the monotony, futility, alienation, and work-induced sicknesses experienced by these people . . . Liu and her colleagues started lay-led 'factory fellowships' within the factories."[9]

Closing Thoughts

Jesus was referred to as many things in the Gospels. In Luke he is characterized as a "friend of sinners." This was not meant as a compliment. As a matter of fact, it was part of the reaction the religious leaders had toward Christ and his tendency to go where the sinners were. It was one thing to call a tax collector named Levi to follow him; it was another thing to go to his home.

Luke 5:29–31 gives us a perspective on what we might face as we move outside the religious mainstream: "Then Levi held a great banquet for Jesus at his house, and a large crowd of tax collectors and others were eating with them. But the Pharisees and the teachers of the law who belonged to their sect complained to his disciples, 'Why do you eat and drink with tax collectors and "sinners"?' Jesus answered them, 'It is not the healthy who need a doctor, but the sick. I have not come to call the righteous, but sinners to repentance.'"

The Breaking the Code Challenge

1. If the code is to be broken in your community, what are some new types or expressions of church that need to be considered?
2. Who are specific people living in your community that may require a new expression of church?
3. What practical steps can your church take in order to reach people groups, population segments, and/or cultural environments?

Chapter 9

Spiritual Formation and Churches that Break the Code

"Truth is not a set of rules to be obeyed, mysteries to be known or evidences to be mastered, but Christ, by whom we know and are known. Truth is not discovered, it is revealed in relationship to both the head and the heart. Therefore, Truth is not something merely known or proclaimed but Someone experienced, tasted, and seen as the Psalmist says, by grace, faith, and presence that not merely knows the Truth but loves Him."

Pastor Mark Driscoll, Mars Hill Church

ANSWERING THE QUESTION, "WHAT DOES it mean to be a follower of Jesus Christ?" is foundational to any discussion related to church. When Jesus began his public ministry, he challenged those who would join him in his mission with various expressions of "come, follow me" (Matt. 4:18–22; 9:9).

We love the Great Commission. We think it is more than just a command of Jesus to individual believers; it is a theological mandate for the church. Following his death and resurrection, Jesus prepared his disciples for his departure with these words: "All authority in heaven and on earth has been given to me. Therefore go and make disciples of all nations, baptizing them in the name of the Father and of the Son and of the Holy Spirit, and teaching them to obey everything I have commanded you. And surely I am with you always, to the very end of the age" (Matt. 28:18–20). It becomes very clear very quickly that we are called to "follow him" and "go make disciples of all nations." If this is the case, then three key issues must be discussed if we are to break the code. They are:

1. What does it mean to "go" in today's context?
2. What does it mean to "make disciples"?
3. What does mean to "make disciples" of "all nations"?

"Go"

Going is perhaps one of the most misunderstood terms in the Bible. The church is to be in the world but not of it. Unfortunately, we can often be characterized by being of the world, but not much in it.

The word *go* in the text is the aorist participle *pareuo* in the Greek and carries with it the idea of "while you go," "in your going," and/or "as you go." This is not to say that personal travel was not important to the early church. It was a key part of every believer's behavior, and by the end of the first century, the gospel had spread widely without any intentional strategy. The church recognized that its primary mission was to "go and make disciples" of all nations.

The evangelistic model of the early church was more similar to that of Jesus as illustrated by his encounter with the woman at the well. It looked a lot less like many of the modern programmatic forms that many churches now employ. In John 4, Jesus encountered a Samaritan woman at a well and had a very personal spiritual encounter with her. As a result of this personal encounter, she went back to the village and we see how people in Jesus' day came to encounter him for themselves:

> Many of the Samaritans from that town believed in him because of the woman's testimony, "He told me everything I ever did." So when the Samaritans came to him, they urged him to stay with them, and he stayed two days. And because of his words many more became believers. They said to the woman, "We no longer believe just because of what you said; now we have heard for ourselves, and we know that this man really is the Savior of the world" (John 4:39–42).

A pattern emerges that is consistent throughout the entire New Testament. It involves three things: (1) people have a personal encounter with Jesus Christ, (2) they go back to their own community or *"oikos"* and tell those around them, and (3) those who hear go and explore for themselves the things they have seen and heard. This is the approach that many effective churches use to create a culture for life change.

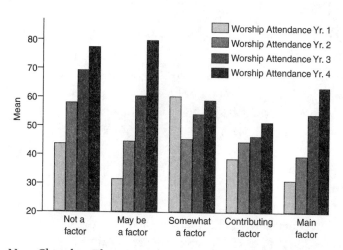

New Churches That Consider Evangelism Training a Factor in Their Growth Are Smaller Than Those That Do Not

Ironically, it is often when we train people to do evangelism that they become less effective in the process. One of the findings of my (Ed's) study of 601 church planters was that those who considered evangelistic training an essential part of their growth were actually fewer than those who did not.

In my study, I explained: "One counterintuitive factor related to 'Evangelism Training Programs.' When churches consider evangelism training as a key factor, they are smaller than those that do not. . . . Perhaps churches that emphasized evangelism training were programmatic in their approach, and they struggled with relational evangelism." (See graph on page 121.)

The statistics may help explain that part of going is relational, not the memorization of certain presentations and strategies.

The church is God's primary instrument for communicating the Good News. The church is God's missionary to the world. There is nothing more important related to fulfilling the Great Commission than a church which understands that this commission is central to its mission, has structured its ministry around the centrality of this mission, has created an environment that welcomes outsiders into this mission, and deploys insiders in fulfilling this mission. This became very evident in the first church.

In Acts 2 and following, we see that the disciples made the temple courts their public meeting place for proclaiming the gospel while they gathered regularly in homes for "the apostles' teaching and to the fellowship, to the breaking of bread and to prayer" (Acts 2:42). It was within this context that the gospel flowed freely and moved quickly throughout the known world.

In Acts 8 the early church began to "settle down." God used persecution to continue to move the early church beyond its comfort zone. In verse 1 we read, "On that day a great persecution broke out against the church at Jerusalem, and all except the apostles were scattered throughout Judea and Samaria." Then in verse 4, "Those who had been scattered preached the word wherever they went."

If it is true that God has sent Christ and Christ has sent the church, then we must take seriously the fact that the church is God's instrument for mission. In light of this, the activities of the early church make even more sense. They had a large group environment where those outside the church might be exposed to the gospel and a small group structure where those who were moving into the church through faith in Christ might be equipped to make this mission central to their lives.

The principle is this: Those outside the church need a safe place and safe people to help them on their journey toward faith. In cultures like ours, simultaneously pre-Christian and post-Christian, life change is a process that often involves conversion from a radically different worldview to a biblical one. In some cases, that conversion can be instantaneous. In most cases, God draws people to himself through a journey that includes making connections with a Christian community.

I (Ed) tried to capture that reality graphically in the "Evangelism Journey." I provided a generic example of how people come to Christ in community. Evangelism is a journey involving stages or steps. It is more than just a neat linear process, but it is usually a journey in community.

There are two conversions—one temporal and one eternal. The first conversion is the *conversion to community*. With few exceptions, people come to Christ after they have journeyed with other Christians—examining them and considering their claims. They can come into community at any point. Thus, the funnel-shaped lines (representing community) stretch all the way to the top of the diagram. At any point, a person can decide to begin a spiritual journey toward Christ.

The circle represents the church. Church and Christian community must not be the same thing. Unbelievers can and should be invited into the community, but they cannot be part of the church. A church is a body of believers (more on that later). A person becomes part of the church with the second and eternal conversion, *the conversion to Christ*.

Each curved arrow is representative of evangelism. For example, a person who has rejected God and who is living in rebellion can be challenged to live a different kind of life by a committed believer. In this context, the lost person can decide to consider the validity of a just God in conversation with his Christian friends. He may begin to believe that God is real and may then consider the claims of Christ. At some point, he begins to consider these things in community with believers.

Earlier we suggested that this conversion takes place over time and often is the result of experiences, services, and community. With this in mind, the church must become a safe place for people to experiment with and experience different aspects of the Christian faith. As such, followers of Christ must have a heart for engaging and loving people of different values, experiences, and worldviews. They must also be equipped to engage people who are both far away and near to Christ. When followers of Christ have the heart and understand how to love and engage those on the "outside," along with a safe place for people to experiment with the Christian faith, life change becomes part of the culture.

Those outside the church most often begin their journey toward Christ with their backs toward the gospel—they either have a neutral or hostile attitude toward the church. Therefore, creating a safe place for people to experiment with the Christian faith is crucial. Over a decade ago, George Hunter began informing us that secular people had "no Christian memory" and that the church no longer enjoyed a "home court advantage." He went on to define those with no Christian memory as "ignostics."[1] We can no longer assume that people understand some of the basics of the Christian message.

In most cases, secular people are ignorant of the gospel. Some are offended by it. Those who are not offended are often neutral because they have no basic understanding of Christianity. Many, and in some communities most, people have never walked into a church, they have no familiarity with Scripture, and they have no relationships with authentic followers of Christ. Any perceptions they might have are skewed by the media.

God is at work in the lives of those outside the church and invites us to join him. It is encouraging to understand that God is more interested in the eternal well-being of people than we are. He has created people with an incredible appetite for him, and he is actively at work in their lives drawing them to himself. His invitation for us is to join him in his activity in people's lives. The key to this is becoming sensitive to what God is doing in the lives of those all around us.

Those outside the church are open to spiritual matters. Some theologians, pastors, and futurists have publicly proclaimed that we are in a third spiritual awakening. The only difference between this awakening and previous ones is that it is not Christian in nature. While all of the polls indicate that belief in God and prayer is up, biblical Christianity continues to decline in North America. However, people are incredibly open to engaging in spiritual practices and having spiritual conversations. For churches willing to employ missional and relational strategies, this is good news.

Those outside the church are most often reached relationally. Most of us have been in settings where someone asked, "How many of you here became a follower of Christ because of a relationship you had with another Christian?" Typically, 80 to 90 percent of the people will raise their hands. This forces those of us who are followers of Christ to be intentional about the relationships we build and the people we engage. While programmatic forms of evangelism like revivals, visitation, and confrontational evangelism have become less effective among many of the cultural groups of North America, there has never been a time when the church needed to be more intentional about building relationships with those outside the church.

Prayer is an essential part of the conversion process for those outside the church. With this awakening of spirituality has come a tremendous openness to prayer. Like many missional strategies, churches that are impacting lost culture are teaching people the eternal importance of prayer. As individuals connect relationally with those outside the church, they are discovering over time that they become open to prayer. When this happens and followers of Christ intentionally begin to pray for very specific needs like job losses, illnesses, and other critical issues, those being prayed for are encountering the God who answers prayers.

Recently, I (David) was in a setting where someone who is yet to become a follower of Christ got up and told her "prayer story." (As of this writing, she is still not a believer.) Her husband was diagnosed with a very aggressive cancer, and many Christians had agreed to pray for him. He was later diagnosed by the doctor as having an "extremely unusual response to treatment." That is "doctor speak" for him being healed.

The woman sharing the story was explaining how this had made an impact on her life even though she was not yet a follower of Christ—but she was definitely open. The interesting thing is that she shared her story in a missions meeting where she was being trained for a mission trip to South Africa, where she would be doing humanitarian efforts with a Christian organization. This is a simple example of what is becoming the norm in many missional churches.

Those outside the church must overcome identifiable barriers in their journey toward the gospel. In a Christian culture, even those outside the church have a positive disposition toward Christ and his church. However, in a pre-Christian or post-Christian culture, this positive predisposition does not exist for the church. A number of identifiable barriers have to be addressed to create an environment for life change. We identified these barriers earlier as image, language, culture, religion, and lifestyle.

"Going and making disciples of all nations" is more than simply approaching people who are already convinced and getting them to sign a membership covenant; it involves an intentional process.

Early in our ministries, both of us thought that the central task of the church was the practice of evangelism. We knew all the approaches to sharing the gospel with others. We knew how to use a tract, the Roman Road, Four Spiritual Laws, and on and on. We were both effective at confronting people with the gospel and getting them to pray a prayer of acceptance. We both grew churches known for evangelistic outreach.

After several years of such outreach with hundreds of conversions, comparatively few remained in the faith. Understanding that the Great Commission is not simply about evangelism makes all the difference. Over time, we changed our strategies and have seen hundreds more come to trust in Jesus Christ—but this time in and through community. The difference is that most of these people have a meaningful relationship with Jesus today. They were not simply converts; they became devoted followers of Christ. Our understanding of what it means to go and make disciples makes all the difference in the world.

What Does It Mean to "Make Disciples"?

Earlier we gave a basic definition of what it means to be a devoted follower of Jesus Christ. Our description included living like Jesus lived, loving like Jesus loved, and leaving what Jesus left behind.

Defining disciple is one thing; the bigger issue is how to intentionally develop people who become devoted followers of Jesus.

The following chart can be helpful when it comes to understanding what it means to be a devoted follower of Christ. This chart includes five stages with each including the following three things:

1. a description of where people are in relationship to Jesus,
2. a description of major barriers they must overcome to progress, and
3. a description of basic commitments they must make to continue to progress.

Our model is not intended to be a "cure-all" for making disciples but rather an example of the types of processes we must think through if we are going to effectively break the code and ultimately fulfill the Great Commission. Perhaps the best place to begin is with the end in mind. The following chart will help.

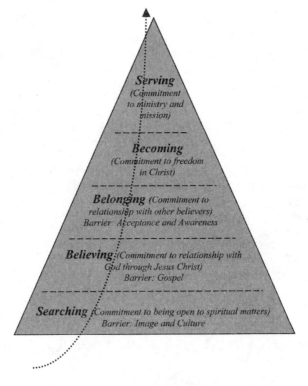

While this chart shows a progression from one stage to another, we have all come to realize that the way disciples are made is not always linear. Often a person will not move systematically from one stage to another. The process is much more organic in nature. That kind of overlap can be represented where the relationship to each function is better illustrated:

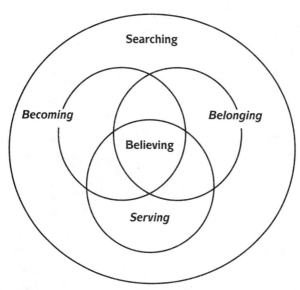

Searching

Searching is the first function represented on both diagrams. Augustine explained, "My heart is restless until it finds its rest in thee." God draws men and women to himself by working in their hearts—drawing them toward himself. In this search, we need to recognize that in today's culture there are at least two central barriers; they are image and culture.

If the church is to be God's light to the world, then it becomes obvious that many people struggle with what they see in the church. In other words, the church has an image problem. Common complaints that those wage outside of the church is that church is boring, irrelevant, judgmental, and arrogant.

The second barrier is culture. If and when a person engages the church as a means of finding spiritual direction, he struggles at the point of culture. Those outside the church often feel like they have arrived at a convention of aliens when they attend their first church service. They simply do not understand what is taking place. It is as if the church speaks an entirely different language.

The challenge is twofold. First, we must address our image problem if we are to engage those outside the church. Doing business as usual is simply not acceptable. Second, the challenge is to contextualize the language, expressions, and forms of the church in such a way that those on the outside can engage in a meaningful way. This will enable them to explore the claims of Christianity and meet their need for spiritual meaning.

This twofold process happens when those *outside* the church meet an authentic follower of Christ *outside* the church. If this follower of Christ participates in a community of faith that makes it its business to engage the lost culture in a relevant way, then a safe place is often provided for him or her to explore the claims of Christ. If, on the other hand, there is no safe place, barriers are reinforced and no journey begins, or if the journey has begun, it ends prematurely.

In order for those disconnected to begin to move in an intentional direction toward Christ, a basic commitment must take place. He or she must become open to the fact that Jesus is the way to spiritual meaning and purpose. Many people are willing to be open to God, but they struggle at this point of commitment to Jesus Christ. Jesus as "the only way" plays right into the idea that Christianity is narrow and arrogant. If they are open to God, then the first major commitment for them is to be open to the possibility that Jesus is indeed God's way for salvation, or in other words, the one and only way.

In a conversation I (David) had with someone not yet a believer, he asked me, "Can I believe in God, but not Jesus?" I replied, "That's a great place to begin, but if you can believe in God, then let me challenge you to pray the following prayer: 'Dear God, I believe in you, and if Jesus is indeed your way for me and all people, then show me.

I'm open.'" After a number of months my friend became a devoted follower of Christ.

Believing

Without a commitment to being open to Jesus Christ as the one and only way, there can be no true Christian commitment. When one becomes open to this possibility, it is often only a matter of time before one embraces Jesus as the one and only way. Yet, in a world where people begin their search with their "backs turned," it takes time for them to move toward Christ. Churches that break the code have realized that they need to provide culturally relevant forms of church that allow people to *progress* toward total commitment.

The believing function involves people coming to a point where they can fully embrace the reality that Jesus is the one and only way; they are willing to commit their entire life to him as their way. The gospel itself is the major barrier. The Christian gospel is the gospel of grace. There is nothing you can do to earn or deserve it. All you can do is simply embrace it, and even that takes ability only provided by God.

When you embrace the gospel, you are responding to God's work of grace, and he gives you all the privileges of full sonship and daughterhood. It is different from other religions or expressions of faith in that it is a free gift. What you do to achieve it serves no purpose. You receive it at no cost to yourself. It is different from other religions in that other religions are about what man can do to gain God's approval. Christianity is about what God did for man through Christ in order to give us unconditional approval and acceptance. Therefore, as Paul suggests, the gospel is the stumbling block that only the Spirit can ultimately overcome—although he uses us in the process.

It is important to note, as represented in the second chart above, that believing is central to what it means to be a fully devoted follower of Christ. However, while it is central, it is often the result of people belonging, becoming, and impacting in the context of their searching.

Currently, where I (David) serve, about 50 percent of the people attending could be described as pre-Christian. Over the next twelve months, we will see about 25 percent of these people become followers of Christ. Most of them will have some kind of habit of personal growth, participate in biblical community, use their gifts, give of their resources, and participate in some kind of impact outside the church by the time they have come to what we call conversion. Obviously, new life and meaning will be infused into their behavior, but a solid foundation will have been laid. As a result of this process, very few of them will depart or leave the faith.

Belonging

In reality they may already be a part of the community, but once they "become" they are now ready to belong at a whole new level. Someone once suggested that Jesus is rude, in that when he comes into your house, he brings his entire family. In an Eastern culture you convert to community; however, in a Western culture conversion is a far more individualized process. Therefore, belonging is an important part of the discipleship process. It is impossible to be in a healthy relationship with God and not be in a healthy relationship with others. Frankly, those who attempt to be in a healthy relationship with God but not others most often fall out of faith about as quickly as they fall into faith.

The good news is that many new forms and expressions of church pay close attention to relationships in the conversion process. When conversion takes place, those coming into Christian faith are already in meaningful community and are far more unlikely to fall away. When this does not happen, the major barriers are often awareness and acceptance—awareness in the sense that those coming into faith are simply not aware that they need to belong in meaningful community with others while those who are in community are less likely to accept those coming in.

The commitment that allows a person to overcome this barrier is not simply to belong to Jesus but also to belong in a healthy relationship with others. This can take on a variety of expressions, but churches that are committed to developing disciples must be intentional about incorporating new believers into smaller communities of faith.

Becoming

Belonging and becoming are obviously interdependent, but at the same time, it is possible to belong and not become. When a person becomes a new follower of Jesus Christ, growth is often certain and fast. However, after one has been a follower for a period of time, it is not unusual to see progress slow and even come to a halt. When this happens, frustration and confusion are the result. If this is to be overcome, it is important to understand the barriers that come along with becoming.

The barriers can be generalized as understanding and lifestyle. Most of us have certain lifestyle issues that require major attention in order to overcome. When these exist in a follower's life, it is necessary to address them in a holistic and healing way if healthy growth is to continue. For example, a growing follower, as he is exposed to a new understanding or truth, comes to realize that there are lifestyle issues of how he or she manages his or her financial resources. Because they have "hit the wall," so to speak, as it relates to their resources, they are struggling in a number of areas in their life and faith. The solution is biblical stewardship that begins with repentance. However, it often takes years to overcome debt and achieve certain financial practices that lead to freedom in Christ.

So we see the goal of becoming is to become like Christ in our character and actions, but the barrier of lifestyle can hinder that from happening. Therefore the commitment that one needs to make is to the truth that sets us free or what some would refer to as freedom in Christ. When we make this commitment, we can continue the journey of freeing ourselves up from this world and becoming more and more like Christ.

Serving

Becoming like Christ means to serve others and to give our lives away in doing so for others. Jesus tells us that in order to have life we must lose our lives. Being a follower of Jesus is about giving your life away. Therefore, our commitment is to missions and ministry. One way of putting it is this—as a follower of Jesus, we are on a mission to the world and a ministry to the church.

The major barrier in serving is often a structural barrier. It is not unusual for all of our energy to go into running the organizational church. Therefore, it is important that we develop simple expressions of church that free us up to serve, both those within the church and those who are yet to become a meaningful part of the church. Our commitment becomes one to the Great Commission—coming full circle from one who was searching to one who is serving those who are searching and those who have found.

What Does Jesus Mean by "All Nations"?

This leads us to a discussion on "What does Jesus mean by 'all nations'?" For the purpose of this book, we have defined it in three groups: (1) people groups, (2) population segments, and (3) cultural environments. In order for people to become devoted followers of Jesus, they must hear and experience the gospel in a context they understand. When the gospel is contextualized, the potential for an indigenous church is maximized. When this happens, exponential growth of believers and churches is possible. Therefore in any geographical area there is likely a need for many different expressions and forms of the church. Breaking the code allows us to develop churches for "all nations."

It is important to contextualize the disciple-making process to each specific group. This is a challenge for many existing churches. Since many of these churches were formed when denominational expansion was at its peak, many of them take on a more programmatic expression of church. Now one size fits all. Reaching "all nations" involves a customization of strategy, forms, and expressions to specific people groups, population segments, and environments.

For Northwoods Church in Keller, Texas, their process is called T-Life—where the T represents transformational life. The church's process involves three components: (1) worship, (2) community, and (3) missions. The process that I am most familiar with is the place where I (David) serve, Mountain Lake Church. We employ the five "G's" as our road map for spiritual formation. These are the five processes in which we believe growing followers of Christ should be actively engaged regardless of how a local church expresses them:

- Personal spiritual *Growth.*—We focus on helping followers of Christ discover how to hear God on a regular, consistent basis and how to respond in obedience and faith.

- Using our *Gifts.*—This is where we focus on encouraging people to find a meaningful place of service. For us, it is not an issue of gifts as much as it is an attitude of service. We do not give gift tests and spend a lot of energy on the different gifts, but we focus on developing a heart of service.

- Community through *Groups.*—A large part of the people who attend MLC belong to a group, but it is not simply about belonging to a group; it is about experiencing true biblical community.

- Visionary *Giving.*—At MLC discipleship is measured by whether or not the people are getting the giving part of being a Christ follower. This means not simply giving financially, even though that is a large part of it, but seeing our lives under the ownership of Christ and giving him more of that ownership every day.

- *Greater* impact.—When people are meaningfully engaged in these four "G's," it always leads to greater impact which is the tangible result of living a life fully devoted to Christ. At MLC that means investing in people outside the church and partnering in some type of strategic mission in the world.

At Lake Ridge Church, the church where I (Ed) serve as copastor, we plan a Lake Ridge Journey class that all attend, and then we take them through a series of biblical practices toward maturity. It looks like this:

- Practices of Spirituality (prayer, Bible study methods)
- Practices of Worship (song, meditation, tithing)
- Practices of Missional Living (evangelism)
- Practices of Service (spiritual gifts, ministry involvement)
- Practices of Community (fellowship, accountability)
- Practices of Simplicity (simple living, family, giving)

Each church needs to contextualize all of the stages identified in the model presented earlier. In order for a church to break the code, it must develop a contextual discipleship-making process that pays close attention to overcoming image and cultural barriers.

The Breaking the Code Challenge

1. What does it mean to "be a disciple"?
2. What is your process for connecting with disconnected people and developing them into disciples?
3. What are the steps you need to make to develop a more holistic discipling process?

Chapter 10

Revitalization to Missional Ministry

"We had to begin with who we were and how God had wired our heart. People don't connect with our (church) culture, but with our heart and passion."

Jon Davis, Summit Church

MOST CHURCHES ARE NOT BREAKING through—but they can. Churches that need revitalization need to ask why they are stagnant in the first place. It is amazing but consistent—churches that need to grow think they can do it without change! They think they can break the code by doing the same things they have always done. The problem is, if they keep doing things the same way, they will have the same results.

Instead, most churches need to be led to embrace change if they are going to see different results. For some, this chapter will seem a step back in time. There are many references to things many readers don't talk about any longer. Well . . . that's the point, isn't it? Breaking the missional code also is for stagnant churches when they break through to reach their communities for the gospel. We have had the privilege of leading some churches to change and grow, and we always start by encouraging people to care for the lost more than they care for their own comfort—to embrace change because it helps them to be more effective at reaching their community. Doing the same thing the same way produces the same results. Change is often needed to be more effective. However, people resist change. But if people can see that change will produce growth, they are often more open to changing.

Christians love seeing people come to Christ—they just forget that joy. Too frequently, they have chosen their traditions over their children. They have chosen their comfort over their effectiveness. They are part of that 89 percent of churches not experiencing healthy growth.

Making the Change to Growth

As a pastor or a church leader, you probably already know that something has to be different today to see different results tomorrow. But what change is needed to put your church back on the growth path? How does a church become missional in its context?

Generally, a church needs to address more than one area of church life in order to engage its community for the sake of the gospel. The first area is the most important: spiritual renewal. Churches need to rediscover their passion for God and his mission. From a renewed passion for reaching the lost will flow other areas such as:

- Worship that honors God and connects with the disconnected
- Partnering with believers and seekers to reach the disconnected in a safe place
- Connecting new disconnected people to a faith process

Worship that Honors God and Connects with Community

Churches often rediscover their passion for God and his mission by examining their worship. Unfortunately, some think that "jazzing up" the worship is a quick fix. They think that starting a "seeker service" is the answer. It is not. A "seeker service" in the Family Life Center is not always a sign of change. It may be a sign of resistance.

The solution lies in seeking God's heart and at the same time, finding worship that helps others connect with God. In many cases, the worship of the church was once meaningful but has since lost its cultural relevance. Younger families may no longer find it "worshipful" to sing "here I raise my Ebenezer, hither by thy help I come," so they leave for other places. Also, unbelievers may find themselves uncomfortable, not at the preaching and content of the Word, but with the expressions and cultural forms of worship. So for many churches, the first concern is the worship and how it can simultaneously honor God and connect with the community.

Worship cannot be the end of a breaking-the-code strategy, but it is a good beginning. When we create a God-centered and culturally appropriate worship service, it helps us to begin the process of seeking God for other changes that also need to come.

Kevin Hamm has led Valley View Church from a declining church of three hundred to a vibrant congregation of more than two thousand in Louisville, Kentucky. The church baptized 221 people last year—a far cry from seven years ago when they used buckets to catch the leaks in the sanctuary because they could not afford to fix the roof. Pastor Hamm explained it this way: "We have worked from the premise that worship is the front door of the church. If worship really is the front door, then you have to look at your service. . . . For the first year, we just looked at our worship and did not want anyone else to come. After that first year, we had our worship settled, and we started to reach out to the community."

Here is the process that we use to help churches experience different styles of worship. If you are a pastor, you might try to lead your church through a similar process so they can break the code to find worship that connects.

1. Make a list of the fastest-growing, biblically faithful, and culturally engaged churches in the area, and go visit them.

In other words, start with those who are breaking the code. On different occasions, we asked the members of stagnant churches to go visit the fastest-growing churches in the area. So far, every member has come back, but they came back wanting some of what they saw! They saw churches that were breaking the code and wanted to experience the same excitement in their own churches. Pastors and church leaders can tell the story all day, but a live picture is worth a thousand words.

To make that happen, give members some guidance on what to look for when they attend. I have created such a "checklist page" at www.comebackchurches.com/resources.htm to help people look for the right things. One of our favorite parts of church revitalization is to hear the reports of longtime church members who come back saying, "The church changed, and nobody told us." When you see the code broken, sometimes you are willing to try a new key!

Invariably, they come back with several observations:

- Some churches are growing by reaching unchurched people, but they generally look different from most other churches. For example, almost all growing churches have a culturally relevant outreach strategy; almost all declining churches do not.
- Churches that are breaking the code have certain things in common but generally only with each other and not with the stagnant churches. People often report that changing to be more like these churches may be easier than they initially thought.

- The growing churches rarely fit the stereotype that the visitors from the stagnant churches had expected: sold out to worldliness and marketing. The result is that church leaders usually can overcome their previously held objections to the methods used by breaking-the-code churches.

One note of caution: pick churches from your faith tradition and find some way to screen them. You want churches that are theologically sound and focus on Word-based preaching but are reaching people in a way that your church is not. Our experience is that the best examples are churches:

- With more than one hundred in attendance.
- That have grown at least 20 percent in each of the last three years.
- That are not known for any major negative issues (of course, just growing gets you a negative reputation with some stagnant churches!).

Be careful not to pick churches that simply fit your agenda. Instead, pick the five that are growing the fastest so that the people trust the process. If you rule out a church because of its preaching or views, tell your people why.

So think of this as an exercise in reconnaissance, like the spies in the book of Numbers, but in this case, they are scoping out what the challenges are as well as what God is doing in healthy, growing churches.

2. Lead the church to experience different kinds of worship.

Begin by leading a church through what we call "a worship experience." For four weeks, the church gets to experience different types of music styles and formats during worship. The churches that I (Ed) have led through this process have tended to be older churches. To get them to experience things in a manner they could understand, we did not pick every style of worship. We focused on a few and progressed as follows:

- Week 1: Traditional. Worship using only hymns, with a doxology and closing with a benediction.
- Week 2: Blended Traditional. Worship using hymns and slow choruses (most churches are now "blended traditional," so it is the "new" traditional).
- Week 3: Blended Contemporary. Worship using a contemporized hymn, some fast choruses where people clap along, and some slower worship choruses. Also introduce some other elements such as name tags, communication cards, and offering at the end of the service. In two cases, we also wore more casual clothing.
- Week 4: Contemporary. Worship using a group of contemporary upbeat songs that people clap to and slower songs that people focus through.

Many churches are discovering the value that other biblically discerning expressions can bring. One recent study found that churches are embracing contemporary methodologies to make them more effective at reaching the lost.

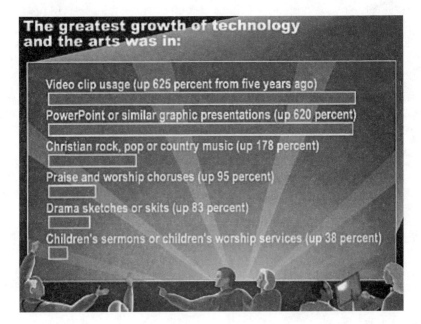

The greatest growth of technology and the arts was in:

Video clip usage (up 625 percent from five years ago)

PowerPoint or similar graphic presentations (up 620 percent)

Christian rock, pop or country music (up 178 percent)

Praise and worship choruses (up 95 percent)

Drama sketches or skits (up 83 percent)

Children's sermons or children's worship services (up 38 percent)

It's important to note that you may not find what you think. According to a study by Ellison Research, "Churches moving toward more contemporary worship styles are outpacing those moving to more traditional styles by an 11-to-1 margin; however, this does not mean it will be effective everywhere. Many emerging churches are embracing more liturgical forms of worship while many churches are finding that Southern Gospel music helps them to relate in their context. As you start the journey to evangelistic effectiveness, be willing for God to stretch you in new ways."[1]

If your community is most effectively reached in a Blended Traditional service, then learn some things from the other churches and do it well. If it is Contemporary and your church is really willing to do what it takes, then make the shift. Be willing to do whatever it takes to break the code of lostness, not just do what you enjoy—or you think the people should enjoy!

This is exactly what code-breaking churches do. They worship God in the cultural expression of their context. As we researched for this book we found code-breaking churches all across North America that worshiped to incredibly diverse styles of music, in a wonderful diversity of places. The key, regardless of the genre of worship, was being able to worship in a familiar way that allowed them to express their heartbeat.

3. Bring it home and discuss it.

What then? Have a family meeting with the entire church. Let the entire church have ownership of the process. Ask some hard questions such as:

- What are these churches doing and why is it working?
- What is our church doing and why is it not working?
- What can we learn from these churches?
- What can we try in our church that we saw them doing?

It is not a cure-all, but visiting other churches and having a local church worship experiment allows your church to experience what growing churches look like and to get a feel for what it could be like in their church. There is no more powerful apologetic for change than to see a church, very different from yours, that is reaching people when you are not. The process enables you to take the first steps to lead the church to a more culturally relevant and evangelistically effective worship.

Partnering with Believers to Reach the Disconnected in a Safe Place

We have all seen poor attempts at evangelism—like a picture in a local newspaper of the pastor holding a big leather Bible with light shining down from above, or a church sign announcing "Turn or Burn." We have seen both, and we are sure that you have too. They produce few results and actually discourage Christians while repelling the unchurched.

If we are to partner with those who are already believers and those who are actively seeking Christ, to reach the disconnected, we must move beyond simply creating a relevant place for people to worship. Since most people come to Christ today through community, experience and service we must connect them with a meaningful biblical community. It has been our observation that for many people and places throughout North America this is some type of large group worship experience, thus we have started by talking about how we do worship. However, unlike *Field of Dreams,* just the fact that we build it does not mean they will come. In reality most often they will not.

In order to see individuals and communities transformed, believers and those who are actively seeking God must connect with those that are disconnected. It has been our observation that those who actively attend churches that are breaking the code are more likely to have relationships with those outside of church culture and are more likely to bring guests to their worship or small group context.

It is important that church leaders recognize that there are at least three aspects of relational evangelism. They include:
- church vision,
- inviting guests, and
- welcoming guests.

Church Vision

Any church's vision for revitalization and outreach needs to begin with an understanding that the church is the best place for evangelism to occur. This is not without debate, but we cannot take the time to discuss that here (see my [Ed's] book with Elmer Towns, *Perimeters of Light,* for further insight).

Evangelism takes place best when unbelievers are already connected with a biblical community. Then, people can make a dangerous decision (for Christ) in a safe place (the church). The church needs a vision for evangelism as a journey in community.

With this in mind, it is important that the church not simply have an evangelism component or strategy, but, sees herself as God's missional agent in the world, bringing life and community transformation. It is in this context that the vision becomes one of fulfilling the Great Commission. Every process, program, and strategy becomes part of what it means to be God's missionary agent to the world.

Inviting Guests

If evangelism best takes place in Christian community, churches that break the code have to find some way for people to find their way to that community. That might mean inviting them to church, but it certainly means bringing them to community. Missional churches find diverse ways to encourage people to visit and then stay. These methods include:
- Helping People Build Relationships. This is more than a clichéd "bring someone." Code-breaking churches teach their members to "invest and invite." They invest in their

unchurched friends and invite them to consider the church and the Christ of the church. *Three Habits of Highly Effective Christians,* by Gary Poole of Willow Creek Church, is a tremendous three-week small group study that can help launch Christians into a lifestyle of outreach.

- Building Awareness in the Community. In many growing communities people are often disconnected from the community and the church. Hope Baptist Church in Las Vegas, Nevada, is an excellent example of a church that broke the code by understanding this. Pastor Vance Pitman suggested, in a conversation with me (David), that people come to Las Vegas from all over the world; they share in common is their absence of relationships and their need to connect. Hope has found success by being that place for people of all kinds to connect. Building awareness into the community can be one means for providing such connections. Many successful churches today have used servant evangelism, direct mail, radio, newspaper, television, door-to-door survey and other methods to encourage disconnected people to come and visit. We have found in our setting that this often works when done over time. Building a positive image in the community often postures one's church to be that place in time of crisis or need. Those who use some type of awareness strategy and expect immediate results are often frustrated by the community's slow response. Those who understand that it is part of the solution reap the benefit of creating a positive image in the community and positive results over time.

A church-based outreach and vitalization strategy without some means of finding new people invariably leads to frustration and failure. Having a church well prepared for connecting but having no one to connect with soon causes the whole system to break down.

Welcoming Guests

For most churches in North America, inviting people into community means inviting them to church. (There are other methods, of course, but most will engage in an "invest and invite" strategy.)

Getting people to come takes work, but making them feel comfortable takes a plan. Most churches have ushers, but ushers are for movie theaters and funeral homes. They need greeters—people who intentionally welcome and connect guests.

First, they welcome guests. For most churches, that means an usher at the door to the worship center. That is expected—but you want to create a safe and welcoming environment. So if you want to really connect with guests, place greeters at four locations:

1. In the parking lot, welcoming people as their first impression (and helping with big umbrellas on rainy days).
2. Outside the outer door, pointing people inside to a welcome center and the worship center.
3. At a welcome center, greeting guests, providing more information, and even passing out name tags. Quit trying to trick guests into wearing special name tags when the rest of the regular attenders do not.
4. At the door to the worship center, handing out church programs and shaking hands (oh, sorry, we were so tough on the ushers, but this is where they come in).

Second, greeters give guests a chance to connect. Let them decide—quit trying to trick guests to wear special name tags, to stand up for greeting, or even to remain seated while people stand "in their honor." People are not stupid—they know you want their name and number for follow-up. If you make them feel welcome and they connect, they will give you that information. If you do not, you may get them to comply, but they will resent it.

Connecting Disconnected People to a Faith Process

When partnerships exist where members and attenders feel confident in bringing disconnected people into your contexts, whether it is a megachurch or a house church, impact can be significant. Frankly, many of our members don't participate in any kind or organized or organic evangelism for two reasons: (1) they don't know anyone who is disconnected from Christ and the church, or (2) they are uncomfortable with bringing disconnected people into our context. Connecting disconnected people to a faith process involves several processes:

- Engaging Guests
- Connecting Guests
- Assimilating Attenders
- Discipling Members

Engaging Guests

It has been our experience that people form an opinion about their church experience soon after they arrive on campus, most often before the first song or the message is heard. Often people arrive on our campuses already convinced that people are going to be unfriendly, the experience is going to be boring, and the teaching is going to be irrelevant to their life. These and other barriers make how we welcome guests very important.

Where I (David) serve we send a first-time card out to every guest asking for feedback. Over and over the response seems to indicate that they have found an inviting or friendly atmosphere, worship music, or teaching. We have also noticed that it is not unusual for the responses of those from other churches to be very different from those who are disconnected from Christ and the church.

Any church that wants to welcome guests must pay close attention to how they welcome guests. Getting people to come takes work, but making them feel comfortable must be intentional.

Connecting Guests

Most churches are large enough that they are too big to connect in the main service. However, in our culture, most people will visit the main worship service before visiting anywhere else. So to connect with people, you have to move them from the worship service to the small group.

Whatever form you choose to use, you need a strategy to connect guests to your small groups. That means your small group leaders need to have an integral part in your small group strategy.

This will require that we walk a tightrope when it comes to this issue of connecting people to a small group. Many guests are simply not sure if they want to take the next step. Moving too quickly can be as damaging as not moving at all, in terms of our response toward new people. Good systems for connecting people must take this into consideration. The best opportunity for getting people to connect exists on campus while they are there in a larger nonthreatening setting.

Many churches recognize this and create intentional ways for newcomers to take the first step. This first step may be filling out some kind of information card. Once this is done, a letter from the pastor is a good first step. It is not unusual for churches to provide some way for people to make spiritual responses on this card. This allows a second step to be made. When someone requests additional information, expresses a desire to attend some class, or expresses a desire to make a decision, the church should have a follow-up process in place that is inviting and affirming.

Churches that are having the greatest success assimilating attenders into small groups are providing additional nonthreatening steps. They recognize that moving from the church to the home can be an overwhelming experience. Some of these churches launch new groups on campus. After three or four weeks, relationships are formed and groups move off campus into homes. Many of these churches are having great success at getting a large number of their adult attenders into small groups.

Assimilating Attenders

Moving someone from guest to member takes two things: a commitment to Christ and to his church (though not necessarily in that order). Sometimes visitors come from other churches, but when they come to yours, your church becomes at least partly responsible for their spiritual commitment.

Every person who moves from attendance to commitment needs to count the cost of salvation and of church membership. Both of these things are best done through a membership class that every person goes through.

Most people seeking to be church members do not understand the fundamentals of the gospel itself. They want to be "good," and church membership is a helpful part. They want to be "right," and membership is a natural result. However, they need to be taught that none are "good" and none are "right" and only the gospel can impute righteousness. Both of our churches make a point of teaching the gospel in our membership classes.

If most people misunderstand the gospel, even more evangelical churches have an unscriptural view of membership. Any church with a membership twice its attendance is not and cannot be living up to its responsibility to care for, nurture, watch over, and disciple its church members. Moving guests from attendance to membership means leading them to Christ and then to the covenanted body of Christ called "church."

Discipling Members

Churches that break the code are not about decisions; they are interested in discipleship. If we have connected them to Christ, involved them in a small group, helped them to commit to membership, and offered real and significant relationships, discipleship will occur organically.

However, every church needs to be sure that every one of its members has encountered biblical teaching on the key habits of discipleship: reading Scripture, prayer, small group, tithing, witnessing, etc. There are so many things people want to learn (end times, spiritual warfare, etc.), but there are some things they need to learn (basic doctrines, basic habits, etc.). These are best done when a church has an intentional postmembership strategy to lead people to maturity.

In addition to making guests feel welcomed, it is important that we provide a positive experience through worship and teaching. Those who are serious about welcoming guests should pay close attention to chapter 7, "Contextualization: Making the Code Part of Your Strategy."

Churches that make these and other kinds of changes are to be commended. Churches can be revitalized or transitioned to more appropriate and effective means of ministry. Summit Church in Summerville, South Carolina, is a good example. After several years of trying without success to gain enough momentum to buy property and build their own building, Pastor Jon Davis led Summit to begin a revitalization process. As Jon put it, "We had to begin with who we were and how God had wired our heart. People don't connect with our (church) culture but with our heart and passion." Jon started leading Fellowship of Christian Athletes and teaching on a local college campus where he had coached football. One day a student asked him, "Why don't you bring church on campus?"

He did, and since then Summit has become a full partner with the college, working very closely with its students, professors, and administration. After one year, a core of about seventy-five people has doubled and tripled. Before moving on campus they averaged about ten students during their weekend service. Now they are seeing several hundred students come through the doors of a campus chapel where they hold their weekend services. They now have a world mission strategy based on international students who coming and finding Christ. For years they had a vision for being a multi-cultural church. Now they are connecting with people's passions. Twenty to 25 percent of the people who attend and lead are from various ethnic groups other than Anglo. The church has truly taken on a campus face. For Jon, a former college football coach, breaking the code required transitioning to a missional ministry that brought the pastor, community, and core together on a college campus.

The Breaking the Code Challenge

1. Would you describe your church as a church with an evangelism strategy or a missional heart? Why?
2. Why is it important in today's world to have a missional heart and not simply an evangelistic strategy?
3. Who are the people that can give you honest feedback from an outsider's perspective?
4. What are your next steps for beginning a transitional process?

Chapter 11

Planting Missional Ministries

"A major part of Redeemer's 'missional' emphasis is to start new churches. New York continues to be the single most influential city in the U.S. (and perhaps in the world). In general, as this city goes, so goes U.S. society. A major wave of immigration is changing NYC from an Irish/Italian/Jewish city into a multi-ethnic city drawn mainly from the southern and eastern hemispheres where Christianity is growing the fastest. This could radically change NYC from a largely secular city at its core to a faith-filled city through church planting."

Tim Keller, Redeemer Church

The Changing Approaches to Church Planting

Methods and models have caught the interest of church planters. Church planters will readily identify what *kind* of church they are starting with a unique vocabulary (Purpose Driven, Seeker,

Emerging, Program-Based, etc.). They also identify what models are not for them.

Many church plants will choose their model based on their most recent conference or the influence of a friend. Too often, we find the models they choose do not line up with the communities they are trying to reach. They have an outreach plan to reach Saddleback Sam, but their town is filled with Blue-Collar Bob.

Church planters who break the code are learning a better way. Instead of franchising the successful models of megachurches, they are finding methods and models that connect with their community. How?

1. *They are learning their contexts before choosing their methods.* I (David) recently asked a church planter what his planting plan involved. He told me, "Don't know yet—have not spent enough time with the people." He reminded me of an important truth: you have to know people before you reach them.

2. *They are learning from others without copying them.* Planters are still learning from innovative pastors, but they are doing so with more discernment. Instead of copying, they are modifying. It is not necessary to reinvent the wheel, but it is wise to see if the tire fits your car.

3. *They are finding new methods and models by learning from their predecessors.* The seeker churches of the eighties and nineties taught us much about how to reach the unchurched. Now, emerging leaders are recognizing that "seeker sensitive" may not mean the same thing today as it did in 1980. They are learning from the models that came before—adapting them to new cultural realities.

Methods and models change as cultures do. Few of us would disagree that some methods from the past are out of date and ineffective today. (Of course, it is harder when others say that our preferred method is no longer effective.) As church planters and church-planting leaders, we need constantly to evaluate our methods and ask, "Is there a better method or model that would reach my community with the unchanging gospel?"

When one begins to see the Great Commission through missional lenses, the mission of the church takes on a broader context. In many communities throughout North America, there are many people groups, population segments, and cultural environments that do not have an expression of church in their language. Even though we speak the same language that our children speak, meaning is often miles apart. At times, the distance between cultural groups is as obvious as the distance between first generation Mexicans and affluent Anglo suburban dwellers. Other times, it can be as subtle as first- and second-generation Mexicans and second-generation Mexicans. While they seem very similar culturally, and one would assume so since they are part of the same household, they can be miles apart. Regardless, when a cultural group has an expression of church that is contextual, impact can often be explosive.

With this in mind we need to revisit the Great Commission. "Our church is open to all people" can be a careless assertion if a clear strategy has not been thought through to impact one's community. In a recent, previous world a Great Commission strategy meant we had our Jerusalem, Judea, Samaria, and the ends of the earth in a neatly defined order. Usually this meant our Jerusalem consisted of people just like us. Our Judea usually consisted of our expanded Jerusalem—people like us but outside of our reach as a local congregation. Our Samaria was made up of people who were within our reach but culturally distant from us. Our world represents those often associated with international missions. Today, this missionary strategy, while noble, can actually hinder the mission.

Things no longer fit into our neat little mission boxes. For years, we have been saying the world is coming to us. At the same time, we have failed to adjust our mission strategies to reflect the emerging *glocal* world. In most cases, our communities consist of various people groups, population segments, and cultural environments. We now live in "JerusaJudeaSamariaEnds"—communities that combine all four targets into one geographical area. And in most cases each group will require a church that speaks its particular cultural language.

Models

A good place to begin when it comes to church planting is an understanding of some of the models employed by churches that break the code.

Pioneering. Churches which use pioneering as their primary church-planting model commission a church planter to go out and plant a church that can be very similar or, at the same time, very different from the parent church. This approach to church planting is usually leadership intensive and requires an entrepreneurial kind of church planter.

Branching involves hiving off a core group from the existing or parent church. This approach works best when the church planter, core group, and the communities are very similar. It is also helpful when the church plant has a philosophy and style similar to the parent church.

Partnering usually involves cooperating with one or more congregations to plant a new church. These churches usually share a common set of values or a relationship with the church planter, but the sponsoring churches exercise no strategic decision-making function. While they provide finances, resources, and prayer support, the primary leadership usually comes from the planting team.

Restarting. More and more today, we are seeing attempts to restart churches for a number of reasons. A church leader in California recently expressed concern that their California churches, planted primarily in the fifties and sixties, were struggling. In many of these churches, the leadership was reaching retirement age and moving back home, which, for this denomination, meant the South. Because the churches had failed to take on a California face, they were struggling to survive. In many cases, these churches need to be restarted and take on an indigenous expression.

In the future, many churches will need to be restarted if the Great Commission is to be fulfilled. Note that transitioning churches and restarting churches are radically different. Churches that are restarted will need to experience death and a completely new birth. This usually requires closing the doors for at least six months. In addition, most often new leadership must be found. This is true for both staff and lay leadership.

Catalyzing churches often create movements of churches that *are* unique, in that they focus on a specific people group, population segment, or cultural environment. They usually set up some type of teaching structure that focuses on the specifics of their ministry focus groups.

Methods

When it comes to church planting there are typically two methods: crowd-to-core and core-to-crowd.

Core-to-crowd involves beginning with a core group of people and expanding it over time until the core grows into a crowd. Moving from core to crowd offers a number of advantages. Because this method usually involves beginning with a core of believers, often out of an existing church, you have an experienced base of volunteers from day one. In addition, you typically begin with a group of givers and tithers that can help finance the mission. If the core is from the community, they will often have a built-in base of relationships.

On the other hand, there are also some disadvantages of moving from a core to a crowd. Probably the most obvious is that existing believers can bring with them church baggage and expectations that are not healthy for a church plant. If the core group is large enough, there may be a tendency to focus inwardly on the needs of the existing group. Finally, existing churched people tend to have fewer connections and relationships with those outside the church. Therefore, while there are some advantages, there are also some obvious disadvantages to starting with a core group and moving toward a crowd.

Crowd-to-core is growing in popularity as a method for church planting. One significant advantage of starting with a crowd is the freedom you have when starting from scratch. You have the opportunity to design the church with the cultural group in mind with very few strings attached. Obviously, this is a great advantage in breaking the code. When this happens, the church can be designed and launched in such a way that it attracts a large number of disconnected people out of your specific cultural group. There are unlimited opportunities for assimilating new people into the new church.

Along with the advantages are some disadvantages or challenges. One of the greatest challenges when you start with an unchurched crowd is that the financial base is likely to be very low. Another challenge is having few volunteers with any ministry experience or Christian maturity. The planter's responsibility is to implement strategies for rapid assimilation and for qualifying the unqualified.

Milestones

In addition to models and methods, a basic understanding of milestones is important if the churches are to be planted. By milestones, we are referring to a significant point when tasks, which signal that an important accomplishment has been achieved, have been completed. I (David) was first introduced to the concept of milestones, as they relate to church planting, in a conversation with church growth expert Lyle Schaller back in 1996. At the time, I was working for a major mission board and asked Dr. Schaller to evaluate our church-planting methods. I still remember our conversation as though it were yesterday. He said something like this, "David, most of you church planters are driven by calendar when you need to be driven by milestones."

He went on to say that we most often launch new churches on Easter or a similar date, regardless of whether or not we were ready to go public. The problem is that when you launch prematurely the church often never recovers and fails to have the impact that it could have had otherwise. For me, this was a major "aha" moment. We had perfected the crowd-to-core approach in the late eighties and early nineties, but we were having problems seeing many of these churches sustain the momentum with which they started. For the next four or five hours, we talked about milestones as a key organizational principle for managing a church plant.

When it comes to planting churches that break the code, "What are the milestones?" Before I answer that question, let me say that we have a bias. Most, if not all, church plants are started by church planters. It is one thing to talk about churches planting churches, but in reality, some planter or planting team is always behind it. Therefore, this discussion on milestones will be addressed from the church planter perspective. The remainder of this chapter is designed to give those who are interested in planting churches or working with those who plant churches an overview of the church-planting process. While this discussion is built on the milestone principle, we have chosen to present this topic in terms of questions every church planter should ask in order to plant a healthy church with the potential for impacting a cultural group.

Am I Ready to Plant?

As already stated, the planter is crucial in the planting process, and everything rises and falls on the planter's readiness. We look for three things in working with a planter that indicate readiness. First, the planter must have a clear vision of what God is directing and be able to communicate that vision. The best church planters are never vague when it comes to their church-plant vision. They seldom start a conversation with, "God is calling me to plant a church somewhere." In most cases, they say something like, "God is calling me to plant a church among a specific people and in a specific location." This vision is most often nonnegotiable when it comes to the planter. We have seen planters walk away from large financial partnerships because they were unwilling to compromise their vision for a particular place and people. This is not to say that they were not open and accountable to others. The best church planters always are, but they are unwavering about their vision.

A second observation relates to their capacity for building teams. More and more today, churches are being planted with teams. The most competent church planters are able to attract both volunteers and paid ministry team members. When someone is attempting to lead and no one is following, it is a red flag moment. On the other hand, when someone is leading and people are following, it is a great indicator that they will be able to attract their cultural group.

A third characteristic that reflects their readiness is their ability to raise financial resources. This will be addressed later, but one of the first questions we need to raise early on in working with church planters is, "What are you bringing to the table in terms of financial resources?" Obviously, it has to start somewhere. But it is our observation from working with church planters that those who ultimately get the job done have a capacity for raising the resources necessary for the task.

Are My Teams in Place?

Having discussed the importance of a church-planting team, we turn our attention to a number of teams that must be in place and prepared before going public with a church launch. These teams are the church planter's family, the church planting ministry team, and the initial group of adult investors.

Church planter's family. For a number of years major church-planting groups have used a behavioral assessment to determine a person's readiness for church planting. This church-planting assessment instrument is built on two principles: (1) past behavior is the best predictor of future behavior, and (2) behaviors are transferable from one discipline to the other. Most of these instruments include "knockout factors." The logic behind knockout factors is that, while there are typically twelve to thirteen competencies, certain ones are an absolute necessity for planting a successful church. Spousal support is right there near the top.

Prior to engaging in a church plant, a planter must ensure that the entire family is on board. Once they are on board, the effort has to be made to keep them on board and provide for their various spiritual, physical, emotional, relational, and financial needs during the church-planting process. Good support systems and a healthy, balanced approach are essential to the long-term health of the church planter and his family.

Church planter's ministry team. The apostle Paul was wise to choose church planting ministry team members and surround himself with people like Luke, Barnabas, Timothy, and Mark, to name a few of the most well known. As stated previously, one of the criteria for selecting a church planter is his commitment and ability to build a ministry team. By ministry team, we are referring to one or more people who feel called to commit their life and ministry to the church-planting endeavor. This may vary from church plant to church plant, but it is never a good idea to go it alone.

The initial group of adult investors. One of Dr. Schaller's original milestones was "thirty to forty adult investors." He recognized that, regardless of where the individuals were in their spiritual process, you had to have a significant number of team players committed to the church plant before you were ready to launch. He went on to describe this group of adult investors as "people who would qualify for any core group" to "people who were way out on the fringe." They were simply people who had bought into the vision no matter where they were in the process.

Have I Solved the Resource Challenge?

A third milestone takes into consideration the whole challenge of resources. Three questions need to be asked when solving the resource challenge. They are: (1) What will it take? (2) How much will it cost? (3) Who will pay for it?

What will it take? In the majority of cases when planting a non-house church in most North American cultures, it will take three things: a start-up budget, operational budget, and salary support.

We are learning that it is generally wise to raise (in commitments not money in the bank) two to three years of salary support for each full-time team member prior to starting the church-planting process. Sometimes the church planter or a team member will launch out prior to raising all the support. We have seldom found this to be wise. On the other hand, other ways can be found for salary support to be provided such as bivocationalism. Whatever the means, the salary support issue should be settled before church-planting activities get started.

In addition to salary support, there are also costs related to start-up. We are referring to those one-time costs that set the church plant up for success from day one. Many partners who are unable to make an ongoing commitment to the church plant are often open to giving a one-time gift for a major purchase for some aspect of the start-up.

The third resource issue relates to operational budget. Once the church is launched, it is important to begin developing good givers and tithers out of the local congregation. While those on the outside tend to give to salary and start-up expenses, those on the inside will be more likely to support the ongoing needs of the church.

How much will it cost? A second question that needs to be raised related to the resource challenge is, "How much will it cost?" A number of issues will impact how you answer this question. First, it is important to understand that it will cost more than you think. When it comes to church planting, we most often have a tendency to underestimate the cost. Many factors raise the cost in church planting—things like cost of living, cost of renting a meeting place, cost for getting the word out, cost of equipment, etc.

Another factor that will impact the cost is where you plant. Since 9/11, there have been an increasing number of church plants in Manhattan. One does not have to spend very much time in Manhattan to realize that if you are going to plant any kind of church in Manhattan, costs are going to be high. Some of these churches have been funded with hundreds of thousands of dollars. Many of these churches are growing and multiplying, but the investment up front was significant.

A third factor is the type of church you plant. Going from a crowd to a core can be more costly than going from a core to a crowd. On the other hand, starting a church among the urban poor will have different cost factors than planting among the urban elite. The form of church used impacts this as well. House churches will be less costly than more institutional types of churches. Obviously, one of the major costs in church planting is salary support. When it comes to salary support, the level of debt that a church planter has will impact the overall cost.

Who will pay for it? This is an important question that every church planter must ask. The reality is that the vision you write you must underwrite. We have heard too many conversations in which the church planter was putting blame on someone who did not come through with financial help. The church planter must take full responsibility for raising financial support.

In doing so, a good beginning point is to understand that people give to people. Those who are most likely to support your church plant will be people who are closest to you. A common pattern that we see emerging is the tendency for churches to provide financial support for former staff members who feel called to plant a church. In addition to people giving to people, it is important to note that big vision attracts big resources. With this comes the idea that "you have not because you ask not." When raising resources outside of your relational networks, it is important to understand that money attracts money. This means that when you have one or two credible partners who are already committing to the church plant, it is easier to convince others to get on board.

Have I Determined the Right Place to Plant?

Determining the right place to plant is a key to long-term success. Earlier, we discussed the alignment factor, which simply means that the potential impact of a church plant is in direct proportion to the degree to which the planter, core, and community are culturally related. When there is a strong alignment between all three, the potential of impact can be significant. Every church planter should look for five things in determining the right place to plant.

Growing population. This is not to say that the only rationale for planting a church is a growing population, but we can all agree that when people are rapidly moving into an area and significant growth is taking place, the opportunity for an effective church plant is great.

Changing population. In addition to a growing population, look for changing population segments. Growing population is often accompanied by changing population, but not always. Many times, the population will appear stable in terms of growth but at the same time will be experiencing rapid change. This is often the case in mid- and inner-city contexts where ethnic transitions are taking place at a rapid pace.

Unreached population. Today, it is fairly safe to say that you can go anywhere in North America and find unreached people. While this is true, many regions of the country and areas within any city tend to be *highly* unreached. The more rapid the growth and change, the more likely it is that the community is unreached.

Compatible population. Most church planters will do best in a place where they are compatible with the population. However, there are certain individuals who have cross-cultural gifts; for most of us, we fit best within our particular tribe.

Receptive population. It is important to recognize God's activity among people in church planting. The heart of breaking the code is finding people groups, population segments, or cultural environments where God is already at work planting or developing culturally relevant churches. Thus, an important question in determining where to plant is, "Where is God already at work among the people?" The more you can answer yes to these five questions, the more likely it is that a church plant will have significant impact.

Do I Have a Clear Vision?

A common mistake that church planters make is developing a church-planting strategy prior to choosing a place to plant. Clearly, it is important to have a sense of direction and a clear calling prior to determining where the church is going to be planted. But if the code is to be broken, it is important that the church be indigenous to its context. With this in mind, several components related to an overall vision must be discussed. The components include values, vision, mission, strategy, and results.

Values. What are the core convictions that drive the form and function of the church plant? This question is the key to our discussion because while there are many things we value, a set of core values forms the basis for our cooperation. For example, the key value we see in many new church plants today is connecting with unchurched people. While these churches may agree and disagree on many things, it is this value of connecting with the unchurched that brings them to a common point and becomes the foundation for cooperation.

Vision. If the church fulfills God's will for its existence, what will it look like twenty or thirty years from now? This question becomes the basis for any vision statement. Vision in this context is simply a statement or affirmation of what we believe God's will is for the church plant over a certain period of time.

Mission. The mission statement describes how we are going to accomplish the vision. While vision is way out in the future, the mission is a reality we live in every day. Mission describes why we exist on a daily basis and what we are striving to accomplish with God.

Strategy. The strategy describes how we are going to accomplish the mission of our church plant. A good strategy defines a process for accomplishing our mission. If our vision is to develop an Acts 2 church and our mission is to develop Acts 2 disciples, then our strategy describes the steps necessary for us to achieve both.

Results. In ministry, it is easy to live your life in the context of what ought to be. If we are not careful, we will spend the majority of our ministry trying to dream up the perfect plan. It is important to understand that no plan is perfect. On the other hand, we need to develop plans that are practical and obtainable. When this happens, close attention can be paid to the implementation and accomplishment of these plans. Results are simply short-range goals that we are committed to achieving.

When these five elements come together in a plan that can be implemented, then impact is achievable, regardless of how formal or informal the planning process is. "The simpler the better" can be an important value in this process.

Have I Networked My Community?

One of the key milestones is creating awareness and identity within the community. The church plant needs to cultivate the community to the point that the community can answer the question, "What niche does the church plant fill in our community?" Imagine if a large segment of the community or your cultural group could answer that question. It has always been surprising to discover how many people in our community have no awareness of our existence, much less why we exist. Networking in a community involves a number of things which are represented in this list:

- determining the spiritual climate and reading the culture,
- creating a positive perception,
- building credibility within the community,
- penetrating social and relational networks,
- building personal relationships,
- inviting people into a biblically functional community,
- baptizing new believers, and
- sending believers back into relational networks with purpose.

For networking the community, this list serves as a progression in moving toward a public launch. In the church-planting process, inviting people into a biblically functional community, baptizing new believers, and sending them back into relational networks with purpose coincides with launching the new church.

Am I Ready to Go Public?

Every church regardless of its method or model, style or form has a public expression. After all, the church is to be "salt and light." When a church plant goes public, it is often synonymous with launching the mission of the church. We are now ready to be intentional about our impact. We have done the hard work of preparation and are ready to fulfill the Great Commission. This public phase is often accompanied by weekly worship gatherings, assimilation, and sending. When going public, a host of things need to be put into place which are determined by the form or function of the new church plant.

For some, it is important to have secured a large meeting place. For others, a house for a meeting place is sufficient or even preferred. Some new church plants require a professional quality worship leader and band, while others may simply require someone who can carry a tune and lead a chorus unaccompanied. Some new churches will require expansive children's ministries, while others require programming for students. The list goes on and on, but the following represents a good sampling of things that need to be considered:

- Is my meeting place sufficient?
- Is my worship leader in place?
- Are my volunteers trained?
- Is all the equipment up and running?
- Is my signage adequate?
- Are all my materials printed?
- Have I had two or three good rehearsals?
- Is my children's environment ready?
- Do I have good plans for getting people back?
- Do I have a good hospitality system in place?

Do I Have an Assimilation Process in Place?

It is amazing. We spend six months to a year getting ready to go public, and then we have six days to prepare for week number two.

Putting an assimilation process in place prior to going public assures a long-term impact. In a new church plant, there are a number of things around which assimilation can happen.

I (Ed) remember watching over one thousand people visit our new church in the first year. Scores came, dozens stayed, but most came, looked, and left. We simply did not have an assimilation process to connect them. There was no system to bring them into the family . . . to get them to a seat at our family table.

The table. One does not have to look very hard to see the significance "the table" plays in the life of Christ and the early church. The "table" meant a place for the Eucharist, but also it was the place of community and family. The same is true for a new church plant. The ministry of hospitality is a big deal. This can happen by serving refreshments as part of the worship gathering, or it can take place by planning church family meals early in the process. The point is this—do not underestimate the impact "the table" can have in the early stages.

Tasks. There are many tasks that need to be done around a church plant. Beyond just accomplishing certain tasks, the tasks themselves are an excellent means for moving new people through the assimilation process. Look for creative ways to involve new people in simple tasks.

Newcomer's orientation. Many churches have incorporated some type of newcomer's event or orientation within their strategy of assimilating people. This gives new people a nonthreatening place where they can take the next step.

Small groups. By far one of the most positive means of assimilating people is through small group involvement. At the same time, small groups can also be threatening. Developing strategies and processes for overcoming this threat can go a long way in assimilating new people. An important question to ask is, "In my context, how can I get new people into a small group?"

Life development processes. In some contexts, a life development process is a good next step. Once again, guests like newcomer events, and classes are often seen as a safe place to take the next step, especially when they are done on a mutual court.

Relationships. By far the best means of assimilation is through relationships. If an existing core can be mobilized to connect relationally with new people, the new church can have a significant impact. Better yet, if people arrive due to relationships versus a marketing strategy, the chances of them being assimilated are far greater.

While there are many other issues related to growing a healthy church that make an impact, this overview allows one to become aware of the major models, methods, and milestones in planting a healthy church. For more information, see *Planting Missional Churches* (the revised and updated second edition of *Planting New Churches in a Postmodern Age*), which was released in conjunction with this book.

One thing is certain: if we are to fulfill the Great Commission, church planting will have to be part of every established church's vision and strategy. Churches that break the code of their community need to send people and resources to help break the code among other peoples—in the same community and around the world.

The Breaking the Code Challenge

1. Identify people groups, population segments, or cultural environments in your community that will require a church plant in order to be reached.
2. How can your church participate in planting churches to reach those outside of your direct influence?
3. Where do you already have a ministry presence that could best become a church plant?

Chapter 12

Emerging Networks: New Paradigms of Partnership

"We had eighty graduates from the seminary, and what are we going to do with them . . . Man, we need missionaries."

Warden Burl Cain, Angola Prison

BREAKING THE CODE INVOLVES BREAKING into prison for Warden Burl Cain. In 1997 he invited New Orleans Baptist Seminary into the prison to provide a four-year college for training ministers. As a result, in 2002 the first class graduated. With over eighty graduates the question became, "What do we do with the inmates that have been trained to be ministers?" For Cain the answer was profound: "We need missionaries." As a result, prisoners from Angola Prison are sent to other state penitentiaries to serve two-year terms as missionaries. They serve alongside chaplains, ministering and starting churches. They have the advantage over chaplains in that they spend 24/7 with other inmates and take the idea of being indigenous to the ultimate level.[1]

Perhaps nothing illustrates new emerging networks more then this partnership between Warden Burl Cain and New Orleans Baptist

Seminary. One thing is for sure, without new paradigms of partnerships this kind of impact would not exist. We simply can't do business as usual and fulfill the Great Commission.

Some that are breaking the code have started exploring new ways of doing ministry in partnership. Groups like Acts 29, GlocalNet, Xpansion, Stadia, Redeemer's Church Multiplication Alliance, Fellowship Associates (and many others) were unknown or nonexistent five to ten years ago. Now, other groups that provided conferences are beginning to form coaching and other forms of networks (i.e., Purpose Driven, Fellowship Connection, etc.). Networks have become a major part of church life in North America. Denominations are still struggling to relate to such networks, but churches are clearly not. In addition to partnering with our denomination, we are both involved in such networks.

Most of these networks have a particular plan or focus. Some networks specifically plant churches for a certain group or denomination. For example, Stadia and The Orchard Group both plant independent Christian churches. However, most are transdenominational—working with churches in and out of other denominations.

Acts 29 explains it this way: "Acts 29 is a trans-denominational peer-to-peer network of missional church planting churches. . . . Acts 29 churches assist called and qualified pastors as they pursue their church planting dreams through assessment, coaching, training, funding, and friendship by connecting them with like-minded people."[2]

GlocalNet describes their purpose this way: "GlocalNet is a network of churches worldwide who have the vision of being a part of one of the first global church-planting movements in history! Our purpose is to form clusters of churches in cities around the globe that will transform the world. GlocalNet churches/clusters are committed to 3 strategic objectives:

- Starting multiplying churches
- Transforming local communities
- Impacting the world through nation building."[3]

We believe that these early networks will open a floodgate of church alliances. Churches will begin to pool resources to plant and support churches based on affinity (and then, perhaps, beyond such affinities). We are aware of fourteen networks that are presently forming. Ministries also exist that specifically help form and connect such networks. Global Church Advancement states its purpose as helping churches and mission agencies to "form regional church planting networks which will intentionally develop *Kingdom Partnerships* with other regional networks (of differing affinities) to work toward the common goal of the spiritual and cultural transformation of cities and regions" (see Global Church Advancement at www.gca.cc).

These affinity-based church planting networks are not without their drawbacks. Although it is exciting to see churches engaged in mission at a higher level, their typical affiliation is by affinity, removing them from fellowship with groups different from themselves. (For example, having been at meetings for many of these networks, I notice that ethnic diversity is sorely lacking.) Thus, denominational structures, which tended to unite persons of different backgrounds, are being (in some cases) abandoned for networks where all the churches are of the same style and paradigm. Furthermore, the kingdom of God is bigger than church planting—but many of these networks are solely focused on church planting or growth. They lack the structures to support orphanages, care for the poor, and engage in international missions (in some way other than the "we will send you money because you know how to impress visiting pastors" approach).

Also, these networks now face the reality of their success. In the recent Acts 29 strategic plan, organizational development issues have surfaced. For example, a recent Acts 29 document states: "Until this point, Acts 29 has functioned as a loosely connected network with informal systems. But . . . to grow Acts 29 to a movement of 1,000 churches . . . we must make the transition from informal to formal systems, and from leaders who function as generalists to a team of specialists."[4] As they adopt church support systems, these networks will quickly begin to look like other denominational structures. That is neither troubling nor a guarantee that they will become denominations (though that is always possible). Instead, it is a recognition that like needs produce like structures and in some cases they duplicate what already exists.

The new model being created by Saddleback Church may eventually have great implications for the North American scene. The P.E.A.C.E. plan has been broadly discussed but, at the time of this writing, scarcely represented on their Web site (and, at a recent meeting for pilot pastors, postponed another year). This plan will be a major paradigm shift with regard to networking for missions—one that will eventually be mirrored in the North American churches. Curtis Sergeant, director of the initiative, explained: "We are still developing the process, and any reference out there is probably wrong. But it will change the way we do missions."[5]

Rick Warren explains (in one of the few references on his Web site): "This is a simple strategy that every church can use to **P**lant churches, **E**quip leaders, **A**ssist the poor, **C**are for the sick, and **E**ducate the next generation. It is a *local church-based paradigm for missions* in the 21st century, and we believe God will use it to bring worldwide revival."[6]

The lengthy quote below, preached by Rick Warren at Saddleback in 2003, reflects the views of many persons involved in these new church partnerships both internationally and in North America.

> The bottom line is that we intend to reinvent mission strategy in the 21st century. . . . In the first century, mission strategy was always congregationally based. . . . There were no mission societies, mission boards, or parachurch organizations. . . . Today, most local churches are sidelined and uninvolved when it comes to missions. The message from most mission and parachurch organizations to the local church is essentially "Pray, pay, and get out of the way." But in the 21st century, Kay and I intend to help thousands of other local churches to move back to the frontline in missions, in compassion, and in providing the social services that historically the church provided.

I believe the proper role for all the great parachurch and relief organizations is to serve local churches in a support-ive role, offering their expertise and knowledge, but allow-ing the local churches around the world to be the central focus and the distribution centers.[7]

Simply put, churches are choosing to network, cooperate, and do missions in a new way. They are not asking for permission to do it; they are just doing it. As a result, these churches are having a higher involvement in transformational mission than ever before.

As these networks grow and gain influence, denominations are trying to discern how best to relate to transdenominational net-works. (Warren indicated that the 40 Days of Purpose campaigns are preparing churches across all denominations to participate.) For many, these alliances are seen as a threat. However, it is hard to dis-miss networks through which more and more churches are finding a meaningful outlet for mission involvement. These churches are more involved in missions than ever before—although not in a traditional manner and not through the preexisting system, whether interna-tional or North American.

Role of Denominations

The obvious question becomes: "What is the role of the denomi-nation in the missional church movement?" If they exist for more than the (very important) task of sending intentional missionaries, they need to consider how to partner with the churches and their leaders. Lyle Shaller comments, "The denominational systems that were designed to serve the clientele of 1955 and to work in the cul-tural, social, religious, economic, and demographic context of that era have failed when the unanticipated became the new reality." The old systems, Schaller says, "collapsed because they were designed to serve a foreseeable set of circumstances." That is what he means by the "new reality."[8] There are four core issues that all denominational entities must consider if they are going to be key players in this emerging apostolic world:

1. *How they define the basis for cooperation.* Denominations that insist on specific forms of programming and expressions of church will be challenged in the near future. On the other hand, those that define their cooperation around biblical beliefs and missions as a foundation for cooperation will continue to have a bright future.

2. *How effective will they be at staying out of the headlines for things that do not matter?* Over the past few years, a growing number of churches have chosen not to align with a denomination due to bad publicity in their denomination. Churches that break the code realize that all barriers must be removed with the exception of the gospel itself—which Paul describes as a stumbling block, "but we preach Christ crucified: a stumbling block to Jews and foolishness to Gentiles" (1 Cor. 1:23). By stumbling block, he is referring to the nature of grace and man's difficulty with accepting salvation as something they cannot earn or deserve; it is simply freely received. It is the payment of Christ on the cross that washes away our sins. This barrier we must live with, but if denominations are viewed as barriers, we will see missional leaders move away from them more and more.

   Standing for morality is not well received by the lost world. But when we are known as Christlike servants, we are known for the right things—standing for the truth. While we think the response to disasters is a great example, our denomination was able to show the love of Christ to people (and in the media), by showing what we are all about.

3. *How effective are they at developing meaningful partnership with churches, networks, and parachurch organizations?* The denominational agencies that learn to "dance" with other organizations can play a significant role in the future, especially if they are willing to bring their resources to the table of other potential significant partners. Networking and partnering is the future. The potential for great synergy

is hard to overstate. Those that are going to navigate the transitions of the church must become effective at such partnerships, networks, and relationships.

4. *How effective are they at adding value to the mission of the church?* Denominations can play a number of key roles to add value to those committed to breaking the code. In short, denominational agencies that catch a vision for local churches and their apostolic ministries have a bright future. Will they have to be reengineered? For the most part, yes, but at the same time, there are several key roles they can play.

Lyle Schaller writes, "I am convinced that for denominational systems to produce the desired outcomes in the twenty-first century, and to be able to do what we know must be done, will require radical changes in denominational systems including moving evangelism and missions to the top of the agenda."[9]

Cast a vision for a new tomorrow. Denominational agencies for the most part have a unique vantage point from which to see the world. Often, those of us who are in the church can be too close to the trees to see the forest. At other times, we are too close to the forest to see the trees. Denominational agencies can serve a vital role in keeping us informed of our progress in regard to reaching the many unreached people living in North America. Someone has to monitor the pulse if we are going to make a difference. Casting vision and informing that vision with real time research is essential to our future.

Lift up apostolic heroes. Denominational agencies can continue to tell the story of real apostolic heroes. At one denominational gathering, we brought in a group of apostles that were pioneering churches among bikers and the urban homeless. They were affirmed and welcomed. They helped expand the vision of our church planting and evangelism leaders. Denominational agencies can serve the church by finding those who are leading the way in breaking the code.

Conduct relevant research. Few churches are equipped to do the kind of research required to break the code. Sure, some of it is intuitive and other aspects are simply Holy Spirit-led. But how do we begin to see the need and develop a holistic strategy for discipling an entire city or region? Who and where are the hidden people? How do we reach them? If we do not know, where do we begin? What do we do with our new findings? How do we communicate with others coming behind us? Denominational agencies can come alongside these apostolic leaders and ministries and help provide good research.

Supplement the local church in equipping apostolic leaders. More and more apostolic leaders will come out of the harvest. We are seeing this happen in congregations like Set Free Church, Yucapi, California. We have referred to them many times earlier in this book. Under the apostolic leadership of denominational missionary Don Overstreet, who came alongside the congregation and pastor to assist in starting this movement, they began to raise up leaders out of the harvest. They established a partnership with California Baptist College in order to develop a pastor's school on the Set Free Church campus.

This school, while it is a partnership, is unique to the Set Free Church and is seen as Set Free's pastor school, not Cal Baptist's pastor school. This is more than a subtle difference. Through this partnership, indigenous leaders are equipped through an eighteen-month training program and sent out to pioneer new churches among this very specific population segment. They are breaking the code as they plant churches among this population segment in cities like Los Angeles, Seattle, and Atlanta.

The old paradigm of leaving one's local church and spending three years to prepare for ministry is becoming less common. Seminary education is important, but new approaches need to continuously be explored if we are going to have maximum impact in the culture. Many seminaries, colleges, and Bible colleges have made great strides by offering seminary extension courses, on-line degrees, seminary extension campuses, and the like.

However, this is not enough! Seminaries must continue to take a very careful look at their role and relationship to the local church. They must continue to ask what it means to equip leaders for today and what they can do that the local church cannot do. Just as churches must continue to examine how they can break the code, seminaries and other educational institutions must continue to examine how they can break the educational code. How can they deliver education to indigenous leaders within their contexts? What do they need to deliver in terms of education, and what should be left up to the church?

Network learning communities and reporting results. No one does this better than Leadership Network, a parachurch ministry founded by Bob Buford. Leadership Network has pioneered the development of learning communities. They find apostolic leaders who have broken the code in a specific context and bring them together. They encourage dialogue by raising the right questions among the right leaders. Then they collect these discoveries and report them to the larger community. Other denominational groups can take the lead in bringing these apostolic leaders together for learning and strategizing.

Provide financial resources for apostolic leaders. There was a day when many denominational models for church planting were that of supplementing leaders to serve as mission pastors in a local congregation. This may have worked well in a church-friendly culture; however, this is no longer the case. New approaches to sending out apostolic leaders must be considered. This approach presents many challenges. How do you provide financial resources for those on the very edge of breaking the code? Few existing congregations in North America are interested in paying the salary of someone to work with a people group that shows very little promise of becoming financially self-sufficient. Denominations can make a difference in this area by providing resources to apostolic leaders who are hard at work breaking the code among unreached people groups, population segments, or cultural environments.

Help leaders move beyond their own ethnic, economic model or other ghetto. Too many of these networks are affinity based—only certain kinds of leaders are there. They have great enthusiasm but not great diversity. Denominations can help bridge the gaps, bringing different kinds of leaders together for kingdom impact.

Denominational agencies and leaders are faced with great challenges and opportunities right now. The landscape of partnerships within the North American church is already changing. Churches and networks of churches are moving in a missional direction. Denominational structures and servants can embrace the present and future of missional church life in North America—by casting a vision for a new tomorrow, lifting up apostolic heroes, conducting relevant research, supplementing the local church in equipping apostolic leaders, networking learning communities and reporting their results, providing financial resources for apostolic leaders, and helping leaders see beyond their own cultures. To do that, denominational leaders will need to ask their churches, "How can we help you fulfill the Great Commission. Schaller explains that our ultimate goal is a "customized evangelistic strategy" for every church.[10]

The bottom line is that churches are pointing to a different future. Denominations need to serve churches to accomplish their mission. The customers of every denomination are churches and church leaders. When denominations are focused on churches, churches will network with them and other partnerships for kingdom impact.

Breaking the Code Challenge

1. What challenges you the most about emerging networks and new paradigms of partnerships?
2. With whom could you partner to break the code?
3. What can you do to help your denomination remain viable in our emerging misisonal context?

Chapter 13

Breaking the Code without Compromising the Faith

"God is true. He has revealed himself in two special and unique ways: in Jesus who came and died and rose again in the flesh, and in His written Word, the Bible. Therefore, we will seek to know, live, and proclaim Truth out of our love for God. Just as Jesus came into a specific context at a specific time, we also realize that our fellowship exists in a specific context at a specific time. Therefore, we will seek to proclaim Truth in the context of the cultures in which we are situated."

Pastor Darrin Patrick, The Journey

FOR TWO THOUSAND YEARS, CHRISTIAN missionaries have been seeking to understand and reach people in culture. In that time, there have been a lot of mistakes. It should be no surprise that it is difficult—it was never easy, and it never will be. But we have no choice. A biblical church is a contextual church.

The gospel is always conveyed through the medium of culture. It becomes good news to lost and broken humanity as it is incarnated in the world through God's sent people, the church. To be faithful to its calling the church must be contextual, that is, it must be culturally relevant within a specific setting. The church relates constantly and dynamically both to the gospel and to its contextual reality.[1]

Many of those involved in code-breaking churches are younger leaders trying to reach their communities. Thus, "emerging leaders" often comes to mean "young leaders." However, age is not the issue that drives them. The issues that drive their passion to reach the unreached are theological and missional.

Theological

Emerging leaders are, by and large, not theologically liberal. A few leaders in the emerging church are revisioning too much theology, and a few in the seeker movement have watered down the gospel, but our impression is that most churches that break the code are solid theologically. (More on this later.)

Some traditional leaders express concern about the level of creativity and innovation in code-breaking churches. That is probably not always an unwarranted concern. However, many of these code-breaking leaders have deep convictions that Scripture is authoritative and sufficient, and they are ministering accordingly.

Evangelicalism has spent more than a century telling church leaders that we must take the Bible seriously. Should we be surprised that many emerging leaders do? When leaders question some long-held traditions based on a scriptural mandate, we should not be surprised—that is the *result* of solid theology.

Code-breaking leaders are asking questions based upon a theological mandate:

- Is the institutional church the best expression of church life?

- Are some rules based more on culture than on Scripture?
- How can we move "community" from a buzzword to a lifestyle?

Missional

Leaders who break the code want ministry options that move beyond the models they have inherited. They have determined that, in many cases, the models of the past are no longer effective, so they are hungry to see new expressions of biblical church and ministry that are effective in reaching their community. They want to be missionaries on this North American mission field. In short, they want to be missional.

In essence, we are talking about their desire to be Christians who are living in a missional way. As a result, their expressions of biblical worship use diverse music, preaching styles, dress, etc. Hipper clothes and cooler music is not the issue. Being God's missionary where he has placed us *now*, not fifty or five hundred years ago, is the issue. Theological and missiological thinking is essential.

The development of a biblically focused *North American* missiology has caught the attention of evangelicals, particularly many leaders who break the code. New models of church have forced the larger Christian community to address issues not considered in prior decades—issues regarding how the church can relate to contemporary culture and contextualize the gospel in its setting.

A church is theologically sound and missionally appropriate when it remains faithful to the gospel and simultaneously seeks to contextualize the gospel (to the degree it can) in the worldview container of its hearers. The most obvious example is the one we explained earlier, Paul and his encounter with the Greeks at Mars Hill. Paul attempted to connect with the worldview of his hearers by understanding and commenting on their religion and culture.

Functioning as a missionary (in a missional manner), Paul did four things in his effort to be missional and culturally relevant:[2]

1. He understood the Athenian position on reality.
2. He perceived an underlying spiritual interest.

3. He looked for positive points within their worldview.

4. He encouraged them to find true fulfillment in Christ.

Throughout the book of Acts, Paul approached Jews and Gentiles differently—based on their culture and level of understanding of gospel truths. With the Jews, Paul reasoned about the saving role of the Messiah and his resurrection (Acts 17:1–4). To the Gentiles, Paul's reasoning was more foundational, addressing issues such as the resurrection, morality, and judgment.[3] In all cases, the culture of the hearer impacted his missional methods. While Paul was the premier theologian of his time, he was also the premier missionary. Today, theology and missiology seem disconnected.

For some people, it is easier to say, "We must not take our cues from culture." Entire ministries exist to attack any cultural influence upon the church. It preaches well (as evidenced by many pastors' gatherings), but it is ultimately both unbiblical and untenable. It is unbiblical because God calls us to our culture and context and, to some degree, the church must reflect its culture. It is untenable because no one lives in an actual Christian environment. Many choose their preferred culture and assume/proclaim that it is God's preference as well. To be theologically faithful and culturally relevant we must be willing to engage in answering the hard questions because the mandate of Scripture and the lostness of culture require nothing less.

Code-breaking churches must be indigenous in their context—and indigenous churches look different from culture to culture. Thus, one would expect that a biblically faithful indigenous church would look different in Senegal and Singapore. However, one must also expect an indigenous church to look different in Seattle and Savannah. Indigenous churches must look different from culture to culture. Furthermore, they look different from generation to generation. Faithful indigenous churches develop their teaching from the unchanging biblical text and the ever-changing cultural milieu.

The problem is that some people go too far and some do not go far enough to reach their community. Leslie Newbigin explains the difficulty:

Everyone with the experience of cross-cultural mission knows that there are always two opposite dangers, the Scylla and Charybdis, between which one must steer. On the one side there is the danger that one finds no point of contact for the message as the missionary preaches it, to the people of the local culture the message appears irrelevant and meaningless. On the other side is the danger that the point of contact determines entirely the way that the message is received, and the result is syncretism. Every missionary path has to find the way between these two dangers: irrelevance and syncretism. And if one is more afraid of one danger than the other, one will certainly fall into the opposite.[4]

To be a biblically faithful and contextually relevant church, *the missional church does not reject scriptural commands, only cultural barriers.* To break the code without compromising the faith requires more than just an attractional technique or model. Too often, the fallback strategy is what we have known (tradition) or what we have heard works (technique).

Overemphasis on technique can undermine solid missiological thinking. There is a lack of theological depth in much of the contemporary church planting and church growth movements because these are movements of technique, paradigms, and methodologies without genuine biblical and missiological convictions. If we do not have a missional strategy driven by solid theological and ecclesiological principles, we simply perpetuate culture-driven models of church and mission.[5]

Though not initially evident, technique may be more dangerous than tradition. The church bound by tradition often recognizes its problem. The tradition-bound church may even bemoan its condition. However, it is often powerless to change it. On the other hand, the church absorbed in technique is convinced that it is missional—that its techniques are actually expressions of mission, while they are in reality methods that *replace* missional thinking.

Another way to look at this is to see that parts of every culture are good and that we can adopt parts of every culture that can be redeemed and adapted, but that parts of every culture are immoral and must be rejected. Thus, many are trying to figure out what is culturally appropriate and what goes too far. The great discussion in evangelicalism centers around issues of compromise, contextualization, and communication.

Compromise

Everyone is an expert on compromise. If you do not do things a certain way, wear certain clothes, sing certain music, preach a certain way, or do certain kinds of evangelism, you are compromised. There seem to be more rules than biblical texts to mandate them.

Evangelicals are struggling with Jude 3 and 1 Corinthians 9:22. Many want to "contend earnestly for the faith which was once for all delivered to the saints" (Jude 3 NKJV) while others want to be "all things to all men so that by all possible means [we] might save some" (1 Cor. 9:22). The problem is that, instead of having important conversations about these things, evangelicals are arguing over forms and methods. Entire ministries exist to attack those who are engaged in culturally relevant ministry.

Yet there are important issues to be discussed. And, yes, some have compromised the gospel in the name of reaching people in their context. Serious biblical reflection is required to break the code without compromising the faith.

Contextualization

The church in every generation struggles with contextualization. What should the church look like? How can we be in the world but not of it? Some have made this an age issue, as if younger leaders want to reach people in culture and older leaders do not. That is not the case. Though many younger leaders have embraced missional ministry, so have many older leaders.

Recognizing this is a contextual issue removes a lot of the argument. Simply put, traditional methods are not bad—as long as they are contextually applied and biblically critiqued in a traditional community. And, for that matter, contemporary methods are not required or even preferred if a community is not contemporary. Contextualization means that we present the gospel and live life together in a missionally appropriate manner. Code-breaking churches are serious about reaching the lost, through innovation or tradition.

Communication

For too long, churches have broken down by lines of affinity: purpose-driven, traditional, contemporary, emerging, etc. If we are going to missionally engage the culture as partners in the gospel, we need a new standard (or perhaps a commitment to our existing standard of Scripture). If young/old, contemporary/traditional, seeker/emerging are biblically sound, and they are reaching people, then we can celebrate our differences. We can and should cooperate with such churches—whether they are contemporary purpose-driven churches, emerging house churches, modern megachurches, or traditional churches.

A serious communication problem is apparent. We know some of the great preachers of the traditional church. We know some of the great young (and not so young) innovative pastors. Ironically, when you ask them, they do not have much bad to say about each other. The problem seems to surface when we meet in larger groups. That is when well-known preachers start speaking against each other with "amen lines" or sarcastic comments. OK, it preaches well, but it leaves us smaller and weaker. We need to grow beyond preferences and, instead, embrace the missional mandate that expresses itself differently in Op, Alabama, than it does in Seattle, Washington.

There are, however, boundaries that every church, regardless of its cultural environment, needs to embrace. I (Ed) deal with this more thoroughly in my book with Elmer Towns, *Perimeters of Light: Biblical Boundaries for the Emerging Church*. Some of the things that emerging missional leaders and churches are doing do not compromise Scripture; they are doing some innovative things that have helped them break the cultural code in their context. There are best practices from which we can learn.

Understanding the Emerging Church

The "emerging church" movement is a dynamic movement and worth understanding for a church that takes seriously the idea of breaking the missional code. *Emerging* doesn't necessary mean *missional*, nor should we confuse *missional* as necessarily meaning *emerging*. Churches can be missional and never be referred to or seen as part of the emerging conversation. On the other hand many emerging churches reflect wonderfully what it means to be a missional church, while other emerging churches like many traditional or more program churches have very little in common with what we are referring to as missional.

One challenge to understanding the emerging church, like many of our church expressions, is that it can't be put into a neat box. To understand emerging churches we must avoid our temptation to lump them all together and to assume they represent one of two extremes—at some evil movement within the church or the salvation of the church. There are serious concerns about some segments of the emerging church. Thus, while we do embrace the desire of churches to connect with emerging culture, we do think that must be done without compromising the faith.

When we talk about missional churches we are not referring to a certain form, expression, model, type, or category of church. We are talking about a church that seeks to understand its context and come to express that understanding by contextualizing the gospel in its community. Over time the church becomes an indigenous expression of the gospel within that culture, eventually removing all extrabiblical barriers. The truest expression of this mission church is that it fully represents Christ in its context, maintaining biblical integrity so that the gospel moves unhindered. When this happens the issue is not what kind of church are you: modern, post-modern, seeker, emerging, traditional, house, etc. Emerging churches that maintain biblical values and missional churches . . . and that is good news.

What is called the "emerging church" appears to have forked in three directions. One fork takes the same gospel in the historic form of church but seeks to make it understandable to emerging culture. A second stream takes the same gospel but focuses on questioning and reconstructing much of the form of church. The third stream and more extreme approach focuses on questioning and revisioning the gospel and the church. For the purpose of this discussion we will look at these three forks through the Relevants, Reconstructionists, and Revisionists.

Relevants

You won't find this word in the dictionary; however, it expresses an important idea. There are a good number of young (and not so young) leaders whom some classify as "emerging" that really are just trying to make their worship, music, outreach more contextual to emerging culture. Although some may consider them liberal, they are often deeply committed to biblical preaching, biblical eldership, and other values common in conservative evangelical churches.

They are simply trying to explain the message of Christ in a way their generation can understand. The contemporary churches of the 80s and 90s did the same thing (and some are still upset at them for doing so). However, if we find biblical preaching and God-centered worship in a more culturally relevant setting, we should rejoice just as we would for international missionaries using tribal cultural forms in Africa.

The churches of the Relevants are not filled with angry white children of evangelical megachurches. They are, instead, intentionally reaching into their communities (which are different from where most evangelicals live) and proclaiming a faithful gospel there. We all know some of their churches—they are biblical, growing, and impacting lostness. This is not to say that there are not some who have taken the ideal of making the church relevant too far. We have talked about the danger of syncretism a number of times—and will say more below.

Reconstructionists

The Reconstructionists think that the current form of church is often irrelevant and the structure is unhelpful. Yet they typically hold to a more orthodox view of gospel and Scripture—the very thing that they say causes them to question much of the current forms. Therefore, we see the increase in models of church that reject organization, embracing what are often called "incarnational" or "house" models. They are responding to the fact that after decades of trying fresh ideas in innovative churches, North America is less churched, and those that are churched are less committed.

Yet God's plan is deeply connected with the church (see Eph. 3:10). God's Word prescribes much about what a church is. If emerging leaders want to think in new ways about the forms (the construct) of church, that's fine—but any form needs to be reset as a biblical form, not just a rejection of the old form. If they don't want a building, a budget, and a program—OK. If they don't want the Bible, scriptural leadership, covenant community—not OK.

Motivation plays a huge factor in the Reconstructionists' approach. When reconstruction results from necessity imposed by culture, government, etc., change can be positive. When reconstruction is motivated and driven by a need to fulfill the Great Commission a missional church emerges. When reconstruction is a reaction to internal distrust, disillusionment, conflict, authority, etc., the outcome can be very different.

Revisionists

Much of the concern expressed about the "emerging church" is directed toward what we are referring to as the Revisionists. Revisionists are questioning and in some cases denying the substitutionary atonement, the reality of hell, the nature of gender, and the nature of the gospel itself. This is nothing new—most mainline theologians quietly abandoned these doctrines a generation ago. The revisionist emerging church leaders should be treated, appreciated, and read as we read mainline theologians—they often have good descriptions, but their prescriptions fail to take into account the full teaching of the Word of God.

Does that mean we cannot learn from them? Certainly not. Many of us read mainline theologians like Marcus Borg and Yale's George Lindbeck like others in the past read Karl Barth—good thinkers, but we differ greatly on certain issues we all hold as essential. We must read many emerging church writers the same way. They ask good questions, but we must find our ultimate answer in Scripture.

Where from Here?

The emerging church can and should be biblically faithful and culturally relevant. But where there is no emerging postmodern culture, that does not seem a particularly missional decision! However, in places where emerging cultures have taken root, there is little option than to become missionary to that culture . . . and to do it with enthusaiasm.

That also has to be done carefully—and not everyone in the emerging church has been careful. We need to think biblically and critically. All our efforts to remove barriers and contextualize the gospel into emerging culture must be filtered through Scripture. The outcome of any of our efforts to rethink, reenvision, reconstruct, revive, and revise must be a more biblical expression of church. When this happens missional impact can be significant and the code can be broken among any people group, population segment, or cultural environment—including emerging culture.

The Breaking the Code Challenge

1. Describe traditions in your context that may hinder your church from breaking the code.
2. Describe areas in your church and mission where you may be compromising truth.
3. What does it mean to be a biblically faithful and a contextually relevant church?
4. How can you help lead others to understanding what it means to connect with culture without compromising the truth?

Chapter 14

Best Practices of Leaders and Churches That Break the Code

"The more you know about leadership, the faster you grow as a leader and the farther you are able to go as a leader. Learning from the experiences of others enables you to go farther, and faster."

Andy Stanley, North Point Community Church

OUR FRIEND REGGIE McNEAL BEGINS his book, *The Present Future: Six Tough Questions for the Church,* with these shocking and sobering words:

The current church culture in North America is on life support. It is living off the work, money and energy of previous generations from a previous world order. The plug will be pulled either when the money runs out (80 percent of money given to congregations comes from people aged fifty-five and older) or when the remaining three-fourths of a generation who are institutional loyalists die off or both.[1]

At the same time the movement of God is like a tornado. It touches down in random, though recognizable, fashion. Places all across North America give us great hope for the future church. In many ways these are the best of times and the worst of times for the church. "For at the same time that we see the demise of one section of the church, we see the flowering of another."[2] We are choosing to focus on the best of times because those are the places from which we need to learn.

Since the midseventies, God has been at work in North America in a unique way; this does not mean that he was not at work prior to the seventies, for God is constantly at work in his church accomplishing his purposes. As the culture began to rapidly shift away from a Judeo-Christian worldview, the church responded in two ways. First, for some and perhaps the majority, the church dug in and took refuge.

"Many congregations and church leaders, faced with the collapse of the church culture, have responded by adopting a refuge mentality."[3] For these churches, it was about survival and preservation. On the other hand, for others it became a time for radical obedience to the Great Commission and a time characterized by risk and innovation. Were these churches perfect? By no means! Did they make mistakes? Yes! Did they go too far? Sometimes! Did they lead the way? Absolutely!

During this time and following, especially in the 80s and 90s, the seeker movement was launched. Not far behind the seeker movement was the purpose-driven movement with its seeker-sensitive approach. Did these movements solve the challenges for the church moving into the twenty-first century? Not fully! But they did move the church outside the box of the 50s and 60s and gave it permission to become missional in its approach. In many ways, they were paradigm busters. The church in crisis found a new identity.

Today, while we still talk about seeker churches, there is a movement that is taking off the shackles of modernity and seeking to be missional in the emerging cultural context. For us, the best way to describe what we are talking about is to refer to this church as the *missional church*. This missional church is committed to being the incarnational "body of Christ" in today's world. It is not that the seeker churches and emerging churches are not committed to this, but the missional church is driven by its mission to break the code. Within the missional church, you will find many seeker churches, purpose-driven churches, traditional churches, house churches, emerging churches, etc.

Upon examining these missional churches, unlike many of the churches mentioned above, they all look different. They consist of many different people groups, population segments, and cultural environments. They express worship in different and unique ways. They preach and teach the gospel from many different vantage points and different communication styles. They meet in houses, storefronts, public buildings, parks, and build their own facilities. They approach spiritual formation and discipleship from different starting points. However, they do share many characteristics in common. This chapter will take a look at the best practices that consistently float to the top in examining this diverse group of emerging churches that are consistently breaking the code.

Leaders Who Break the Code Are Forward Thinking

Code-breaking leaders ask the right questions of the right people. If we are going to break the code, we must ask the right questions of the right people. It serves no purpose to ask the right questions of the wrong people or to ask the wrong questions of the right people. Who are the right people? The right people are the many unreached and disconnected people now living in North America. They are a group of people who have little or no Christian memory. They are people who have their backs squarely turned away from Christ and his church. They represent people who are sometimes agnostic to Christian faith and, most often, "ignositic" to Christian faith.

They are the people who seldom or never attend a Christian worship gathering. They are the people who occasionally show up in one of our churches and declare that this is the first time they have been to a church in twenty, thirty, forty, or fifty years. They are also the people who show up and declare that they have never been to a Christian worship gathering. They are the people who declare that the church is boring, irrelevant, or hypocritical. They are the people who are least likely to be found in the church.

What kinds of questions do we ask them? By now, most of us are familiar with the questions Rick Warren asked his Orange County community prior to planting Saddleback Valley Community Church. They are:

1. What do you think is the greatest need in this area?
2. Are you actively attending any church?
3. Why do you think most people don't attend church?
4. If you were to look for a church to attend, what kind of church would you look for?
5. What could I do for you? What advice can you give a minister who really wants to be helpful to people?[4]

Now, this is not to say that you need to ask the same questions. While these questions are appropriate for some contexts, they are at the wrong starting point for others. Is going door to door the way to ask these questions? Once again the answer is yes for some communities and no for others. Our point is those who are breaking the code ask questions. Stanley, Joiner, and Jones, all pastors from North Point Community Church, remind us how important it is to ask questions:

> It's easy for the needs or interests of insiders to ultimately drive the priorities of any organization. It's just the natural tendency of any group to become insider-focused. If you are surrounded long enough by people who think like you think, you will become more and more certain that's the best way to think. Over time you find yourself inclined to completely disregard the concerned voices of those positioned on the outside.[5]

Code-breaking leaders understand that the future is already happening. Our friend Reggie McNeal makes us think. In the preface of *The Present Future* he states: "We think we are headed toward the future. The truth is the future is headed toward us. And it's in a hurry—we now know the universe is speeding up, not slowing down."[6] One of the ways that we can see the future is through the eyes of early innovators. People thought Henry Ford had lost his mind. The idea of commercial air travel was out of the question. A cell phone in everyone's hands, out of the question. The future is already happening. The next major innovation is already being tested. The next great world leader was born yesterday. The church of the future was planted last year.

We agree with Reggie that the future is already happening. All across North America the future church is flourishing. Leaders who break the code understand this and are scouting the frontiers to learn from everything with which they make contact. At times, they are the paradigm busters. At other times, they are early adapters. One thing is for sure—these leaders are seldom late.

Code-breaking leaders learn their way forward. Learning our way forward is both a discipline and an attitude that requires a reorientation in regard to how we view success and failure. I (David) can recall early in my ministry experience sensing the call to go plant a church. At the time, I was working in a resourcing capacity with church planting and had developed a good reputation for what I was doing. I will never forget telling my supervisor that I was going to move on to start a church. He asked me, "What if you fail?" In that moment it hit me, and I replied, "If I don't attempt it, I've already failed!" It is in this context that we realize that failure is our unwillingness to take risks and attempt those things we feel called by God to do.

Winston Churchill had it right when he defined success as "the ability to go from failure to failure without losing your enthusiasm." In settings that are having significant impact, careful attention is paid to evaluating outcomes and results. This is not to say it is all about the numbers or end results, but there is recognition that we learn our way forward and therefore we must build time into our process to evaluate what we are learning. When this happens, we build a culture where team members are willing to take risks and come up with new ideas. When we evaluate everything on a pass/fail basis, it is not unusual for a culture to be created that is suspicious and lacking in trust.

Leaders Who Break the Code Are Willing to Pay the Price

Our friend Harold Bullock, pastor of Hope Church in Fort Worth, Texas, is a reminder of the incredible price you have to pay in order to be a code-breaking leader. I (David) recall meeting Harold back in the late 90s, just before Hope Church moved into their first permanent facilities after a decade of moving from place to place. That particular day they held their services in the Ramada Inn downtown Fort Worth. Over lunch it became apparent to me that Harold had paid an incredible price, putting the development of leaders and the multiplication of churches ahead of developing a local campus. We both know Harold and have an incredible respect for him as a leader who is willing to give so much to the kingdom. Throughout his ministry he has been committed to pouring his life into the spiritual formation of young emerging leaders. This has resulted in over ninety churches around the world being started by people who have been a part of Hope.

Like Harold and many others, one can expect to be called to make incredible sacrifices to fulfill God's purposes for their life. Breaking the code requires going where few are willing go. Breaking the code where it has not been broken comes with a huge price.

One can expect to be called to the hard places to serve. The easy places are filled with people who are not willing to break the code or implement the code that has already been broken.

What we are recognizing through our own experiences and the experiences of those who are committed to breaking the code is that when you are willing to do whatever it takes to connect disconnected people to God and his church, there is a tremendous price to pay. Sometimes the price is related to misunderstanding and strained relationship. Regardless, this price will cost us on every front. It is not simply hard work, but it all comes with a tremendous physical, financial, emotional, relational, and spiritual price.

Jesus was clear in his teaching that no one should go out and begin a process of building something without first counting the cost (Luke 14:28–30). This is especially true for those who are committed to being an instrument for building his church. Together, we have twenty years of combined experience with planting new churches that are committed to breaking the code. Some have been more successful than others. Some have had greater impact than others, but they have all developed at great cost. Whenever you move outside the mainstream of conventional thought and practice, you are going to pay a price. The question that we must all ask up front is, "Is it worth it?" If we can answer affirmatively to this question, without hesitation, then we are ready to move forward.

Frankly, it has been our experience that many are simply not ready or willing to pay the price, at least not to the extent that it needs to be paid. We can both remember times of reckoning. We were planting churches that required more than expected. Our families were tired and frustrated. We were out of breath. After several years of working through a number of obstacles, there were signs of hope and encouragement. New people were coming and life change was taking place. God had answered our prayers, and the next stretch of ministry would be completely different from the previous one. We recognized that the demands of success were far more stressful than we had thought. We each had to ask, "Am I willing to pay the price?" These challenges come on many fronts.

Physical. When we talk about paying the price, leaders and churches that break the code understand that it is just plain hard work. The challenge will always be how to maintain balance when the demands are so great.

We are reminded of how demanding the role of pastor can be when you are neck deep in breaking the code. Listen to the comments of Lynne Hybels as she discusses Bill's schedule early in the process of planting Willowcreek:

> But Camelot had a shadow side. Not many of us had to spend time there, but those of us who did felt caught between two extremes: a breathtaking ministry experience that gave life more meaning than we could ever have hoped for, and a heartbreaking personal disappointment that bordered on despair. Perhaps a glimpse into Bill's calendar from 1974 will provide a hint about the darker side:
>
> - Sunday Morning: "Church Service" (Bill sang or led the "share time.")
> - Sunday afternoon: "Music Rehearsal" (Bill sang.)
> - Sunday night: "Evening Service" (Bill often participated in these services.)
> - Monday night: "Son Village" (Bill taught.)
> - Tuesday night: "Awana Club" (Bill directed.)
> - Wednesday night: "Son City" (Bill taught.)
> - Thursday night: "Son City" (Bill taught.)
> - Friday night: "Retreat" (or "Team Event," "Overnight," "Concert," "Discipleship"—Bill was involved in all these.)
> - Saturday afternoon: "Tournament" (Bill led these.)
> - Saturday night: "Gym Night" (Bill led these.)[7]

Sound familiar? This is a great reminder of how demanding and how many hats you often have to wear when you are breaking the code. Regardless of what your programming looks like, there are times when code-breaking leaders have to pay an incredible price.

Emotional. Leaders who are willing to leave the security of the familiar must get used to being alone, for it is always lonely on the front end of vision. It is not unusual to be misunderstood and even kept at a distance when you are on the cutting edge of innovation. Shawn Lovejoy, pastor of Mountain Lake Church on the north fringe of Atlanta, Georgia, discusses "church planter's syndrome" or "CPS."

He tells of one specific incident early in the life of Mountain Lake when he held their very first event . . . and no one showed up. He said, "I crawled up into the fetal position that night and cried myself to sleep. I wondered what have I gotten myself into?"

We all have those moments, whether we are pioneering a new ministry or trying to turn around a ministry. There are going to be times that we question our call and impact. It is these times that take a huge emotional toll on us.

Relationally. There is a price to pay relationally. Many innovators drift toward the planting of new churches. When beginning a new ministry, there are often few people around who can provide a spiritual umbrella for the leader and his family. In addition, ministry is simply a lonely place to be at times. The good news is that leaders are learning that they can be transparent and develop relationships within the church. Often, innovators are simply misunderstood. Therefore, if you are committed to breaking the code, you have to understand that there are going to be times when it is lonely. This is not to say that you cannot have and develop great relationships. You can and should, but there is a price to pay relationally.

Financially. We have spent the majority of our ministries working with church planters. What we have learned firsthand is that there is a difference when you collect the offerings from people who come from a highly Christian and churched worldview than when you collect the offering from people who have been disconnected from Christ and the church. It takes years and years to develop a solid financial base when you are reaching disconnected people. This is simply part of the price paid by those who break the code.

Spiritually. Perhaps the greatest price one pays is spiritual. Shortly before Jesus began his public ministry, he spent forty days in the wilderness where he was tempted by the devil. The same is true for pastors and leaders in the church. We all know the stories of those who have fallen. Leaders committed to breaking the code must prepare for spiritual warfare. They must take time to surround themselves with prayer and support. They must submit themselves to a high level of accountability.

Leaders Who Break the Code Build Great Teams

One of the defining issues that we have observed over the years is that leaders who break the code seldom if ever do it alone. Working with church planters, you never have a shortage of people with big dreams and visions. It is the nature of those who plant churches or desire to plant churches to want to be paradigm breakers. However, this thing of not doing it alone seems to be the decisive difference in those who want to do it and those who actually get it done. One of the criteria that I (David) have used to identify leaders is this question, "Who are you bringing to the party with you?" Those who bring no one in the early stages or struggle to get people on board may lack the capacity to lead. Obviously, one of the defining characteristics of a leader is when he looks behind him and he has followers.

When Andy Williams set out to start Harvest Church, he had five lay couples that he had discipled through the years who were willing to leave their homes and jobs and relocate to the Midwest to be part of this leader's vision. A powerful church was born.

Vance Pitman, a code-breaking pastor in Las Vegas, set out to break the code just a few years ago and brought a full staff of four pastors to a major city to establish a new ministry and cast the vision among several partnering churches and had a large number of families leave everything to follow the vision. Today they have a church of over one thousand people in a place known as "Sin City." The pattern is consistent with those who break the code. They are able to inspire people to take overwhelming risk.

In addition to casting vision and getting people to take the journey with them, effective leaders also have abilities and skills in relationship to leading these people. We have observed leaders who have enough charisma to attract people but have no idea what to do with them once they have attracted them. Leaders who break the code know how to build a team and achieve a shared vision. They have the gifts, skills, and experience to maximize their team. We mention this because it is not unusual to find a leader who has the charisma to attract people but who lacks the skills to lead them. Both charisma and skill are required.

Therefore, leaders who break the code have both great vision and good administrative skills. They are unique in that they can see the big picture, but they can also implement the details through people.

When it comes to building their team, these leaders seem to get team members from one or two different places. First, they often get team members from previous ministry involvement. It is not unusual for them to have mentored this person in the past in a different ministry setting. Second, they are highly committed to raising up leaders out of their current harvest location. A few years back this would have been unusual, but today, in churches that break the code, this is very typical.

Jim Collins gives us good insight regarding this in his book, *Good to Great.* He suggests that companies that go from good to great, when dealing with personnel, begin with the "who" before they determine the "what." He suggests that we need to get the right people on the bus, and then determine which seats they need to occupy. This is very much the experience of those who break the code.[8]

Leaders Who Break the Code Have a Different Beginning Point

As we have observed, leaders throughout North America who are breaking the code have a different beginning point. Their beginning point is grounded in a theological understanding and conviction of what the church should be and do. It is not simply about building a reputation, a ministry, a following, or a great church, but it is about a deep conviction that is grounded in the Word of God.

Leaders who break the code in emerging culture see things differently. Many of them are part of an emergent church that insists on rethinking church. Dan Kimball and Josh Fox sum it up this way on their Web site (www.vintagefaith.com):

> There is a rising feeling among emerging church leaders
> and followers of Jesus, that in many modern contemporary

churches, something has subtly gone astray in what we call "church" and what we call "Christianity." Through time, church has become a place that you go to have your needs met, instead of being a called local community of God on a mission together. Through time, much of contemporary Christianity subtly has become more about inviting others into the subcultures of Christian music, language and church programs than about passionately inviting others into a radically alternative community and way of life as disciples of Jesus and Kingdom living.[9]

They go on to describe this new brand of emerging church in the following way:

Vintage Faith is simply looking at what was vintage Christianity. Going back to the beginning and looking at the teachings of Jesus with fresh eyes, hearts and minds. Carefully discerning what it is in our contemporary churches and ministry that perhaps has been shaped through modernity and evangelical subculture, rather than the actual teachings of Jesus and the Scriptures. We need to begin asking a lot of questions again. We shouldn't be afraid to ask questions. Too much is at stake not to.[10]

It has been suggested that "when our motives are wrong, all else is wrong also." Many of those who are breaking the code realize this. For them breaking the code begins with going back to the mission and commission of Jesus Christ. If breaking the code is a reaction of any kind, it is a reaction against the church growth method and formulas of the past and a move back to the basics of the first-century church. Just as the early followers of Christ could not help but proclaim what they had seen and heard, this emerging church cannot as well. Those who break the code aren't afraid of deconstructing the existing church with all of its traditions, programs, methods, and preferences. This deconstruction is not carelessly done, but is done with surgical precision with the Bible in one hand and the mission of the church in the other.

Leaders Who Break the Code Connect the Dots

They connect the dots in the sense that they connect vision with strategic direction and focus. In other words, they see the big picture, define the strategic process, and stay focused. Few churches have experienced the phenomenal success that North Point Church has in Alpharetta, Georgia, under the leadership of Andy Stanley. In addition to being a great communicator and writer, he has surrounded himself with great strategic thinkers. The first three practices in his coauthored *7 Practices of Effective Ministry* are very similar to what we are talking about here; they are clarify the win, think steps not programs, and narrow the focus.[11] We would state it very similarly. Leaders who break the code see the big picture, define the process, and stay focused.

Seeing the big picture. Code-breaking churches get at the big picture a number of different ways, but they all have a clear vision about what God wants them to accomplish. Henry Blackaby is a code breaker. Long before it was in vogue, he was busy breaking the code in Canada. Much of his writing flows out of his ministry experience. Blackaby understood what it means to see the big picture. He also recognizes how you get the big picture. In a book he coauthored with his son Richard, *Spiritual Leadership,* they identified six resources from which leaders often get their vision and then said this about a leader's vision:

> The previous six sources of vision have one thing in common—they are all generated by worldly thinking. This is not surprising; the world functions by vision. But God does not ask his followers to operate by vision. God's people live by revelation. Proverbs 29:18, although widely used, is also widely misapplied. The popular translation is, "Where there is no vision, the people perish" (KJV). A more accurate translation of the Hebrew is: "Where there is no revelation, the people cast off restraint" (NIV). There is a

significant difference between revelation and vision. Vision is something people produce; revelation is something people receive. Leaders can dream up a vision, but they cannot discover God's will. God must reveal it.[12]

Like the Blackabys, leaders understand that when it comes to the big picture of vision, it is not about my vision, but it is about God's will. The beginning point when it comes to envisioning the church that breaks the code is, "God, if you had your way and your will was accomplished, what would this church look like in relationship to the people you have called me to reach?"

It is amazing how practical God's revelation can be. When I (David) was in a meeting with Henry Blackaby, Henry began outlining his strategy for reaching an entire province in Canada. He took a flip chart and drew out an outline of his province and then sectioned it off by overlaying it with grid. He went on to say we knew that it was God's will for us to reach our province and we knew these places were strategic, pointing out several key cities, including a university town. He went on to describe how God had worked supernaturally through different people to open the door to these areas. I was amazed how practical and simple this vision of the big picture was.

When it comes to seeing the big picture, an important question for code-breaking leaders to ask is this, "If God had his way in this church in this context, what would it look like?" "What would this ministry look like five, ten, twenty, fifty years from now?" This is an excellent exercise for any church to do with its staff and leaders who are committed to breaking the code.

Defining the process. Once the big picture is in focus, a second question has to be asked, "How do we get there?" Leaders who break the code are constantly working on processes. For Warren, it is the baseball diamond; for Hybels, it is their seven-step strategy; for Stanley, it is about moving people from the foyer to the living room to the kitchen table.

Regardless of your process, it should serve as a road map for getting to your ultimate destiny. The beginning point should be where the people in your context begin their journey toward Christ, and the ending point completes the big picture. In this case, the process should be clear, simple, sequential, and achievable.

Staying focused. Perhaps this is the greatest challenge in our North American context. Many people who attend church today have been raised in churches that target the consumer needs of believers. Churches that break the code are not interested in consumption. They are committed to meeting needs of people who are disconnected from Christ and the church. I often tell people who are coming to our church from a churched background that this is a great place to be if you are here to fulfill Christ's mission of reaching the world, but if you are here to meet your own consumer needs, you are going to be miserable.

Churches that break the code stay focused on the mission of the church. They have learned to live with the tension that exists between meeting the needs of believers and fulfilling the Great Commission. They have learned to say no in order that they might ultimately be able to say yes to the right things. They are what some refer to as "mean" about vision.

Leaders Who Break the Code Are Constantly Working *on* It and Not Simply *in* It

Our friend Gregg Farah is a code-breaking pastor in Manhattan. The vision for Mosaic Church flows out of the tragedy of 9/11. One would have to do ministry in New York City to understand the demands of ministry in that context. The temptation is to lower your head and not look up.

Gregg understands that if he is going to break the code, he cannot stay in it all the time. He regularly looks outside of himself and his team for answers. He stays in regular communication with those who are attempting to break the code in similar settings. As we have travelled and consulted with churches in urban context, it is not unusual to hear others mention and talk about Gregg and his work in

New York. It doesn't take long to determine that Gregg spends a lot of time outside of his context working on it, not simply in it.

Like Gregg, leaders who break the code are constantly working on it. They understand that working on it involves sitting back and evaluating our current ministry, work and processes, and envisioning the future.

Recently, I (David) met with the president of a major resourcing organization. I have been working on starting another ministry organization and trying to figure out how to get out of the starting gate. On the way over, I worked on a set of carefully crafted questions that I needed answers to from my ministry partner. I never got to ask my questions—he immediately began to talk with me about how we could partner. In doing so, he shared his vision of how they were going to resource ministry leaders.

On the way back to the office, I was overwhelmed by the direction that our meeting went. I was overwhelmed with the possibilities of partnering, but the greatest benefit of our meeting was his ideas. It was those ideas that got me off dead center in my own organization and allowed me to break the code in regard to what I was tying to accomplish. We both agreed that if nothing ever came out of our partnership, the interaction and outside perspective was worth more than gold. By moving outside of myself I was able to work on it. Now that I have worked on it, I can go to working in it. I immediately made an appointment with my Web designer and host to begin to reinvent the organization. It was now time to work in it.

Leaders who work on breaking the code do so in a number of ways.

- *They read.* While a few leaders boast that they have never read anything on leadership, the reality is that those who break the code are avid consumers of written materials in all forms. They read about the disciplines of learning as much from business leaders as they do ministry leaders. They read biographies, research reports, and fiction. You name it, they read it.

- *They seek out leaders who are getting it done.* Leaders who break the code seek to build relationships both formally and informally with leaders who are getting it done. They ask people for their time and are willing to pay for it if necessary. They seek out people who do it like they do it, but just as important, they seek out leaders who do it differently.
- *They use technology.* Leaders who get it done understand the value of technology. They use it to enhance their learning whether they are surfing the Internet or listening to a ministry coach on an MP3 player.
- *They visit others who are getting it done.* A group of business leaders in our community regularly visit other leaders and businesses that are getting it done. Church leaders who break the code seldom live alone on an island. They often spend more time visiting successful businesses than they do successful ministries.
- *They take regular and long breaks from working in it.* In addition, leaders take regular breaks to work on it. They understand the importance of gaining perspective by stepping away from things. They plan study breaks and sabbaticals.
- *They have strategic meetings.* In addition to regular breaks, leaders recognize the need to bring their team together for specific meetings to work on it.

Leaders Who Break the Code Are Interested in Kingdom Growth

Just as leaders who break the code have a different beginning point, they also have a different ending point. Ken Adams, pastor of Crossroads Church just south of Atlanta, who has seen the church grow from zero to nearly three thousand over the last sixteen years. He had this to say: "In the first 10 years of Crossroads our mission focused on being and building disciples. I want to spend the rest of my life being and building the church." Since that conversation, Ken has led Crossroads Church consistently to plant churches and resource church leaders through his Impact Ministries.

The same is true for the Hope Chapel movement. Since the planting of the original Hope Chapel in Manhattan Beach, California, in 1971, Ralph Moore has seen a movement where more than two hundred churches have been planted and more than twenty thousand people worship every weekend. Hope Chapel's main campus continues to have a vision of planting at least one church per year and often exceeds that goal.

Why? This is the greater question because not only do they see the church as God's instrument for kingdom impact; they are experiencing it. In an article written by Ralph Moore he describes this impact:

> God's kingdom is invading our Honolulu. From school campuses to law offices, to hospitals, to auto-repair shops people join together each week to pray for his kingdom to come, his will be done on earth as it is in heaven.

> While Oahu has seen a 30 percent reduction in crime, the curve is much steeper in Kaneohe and Chinatown. Crime in both areas is down by nearly 50 percent since one year ago. Both areas receive regular prayer by organized groups. These groups have touched off a movement. There are "zip-code prayer cadres" on every island in the state.

> We live in the brave new post-modern world. People aren't fazed by logic. They don't care that you can prove the resurrection of Jesus Christ. They are, however, impressed by his sufferings as depicted in *The Passion of the Christ*. They don't much worry about heaven or hell. But they are blown away by spiritual power when it knocks on their door. They are unwilling to debate Calvinism but very willing to participate in an exorcism.[13]

Ralph Moore and other code-breaking leaders understand that the church is a means to an end. The end is the kingdom of God. When the kingdom comes, our mission is being accomplished. This mission is accomplished when other code-breaking churches join together to have greater impact, whether it is through prayer or some other kingdom activity.

These are just a few of the practices of leaders who break the code, but consistently they are the best practices. While they play out in many diverse ways, these eight practices represent the broad strokes of this unique group of leaders. They integrate these practices into their everyday life. They seldom stray off the path of these key behaviors.

The Breaking the Code Challenge

1. What Scriptures and/or experiences have most shaped you as a leader?
2. How do these Scriptures and/or experiences still drive you to break the code?
3. What do you need to do to continue to cultivate a passion for breaking the code?

Chapter 15

The Process of Breaking the Code

"I want to live in the world that if the church is not the revolution that Jesus died to establish two thousand years ago it ceases to exist. I want to live in a world where the church has no more crutches or buffers to guard her from injury. I want a church where a culture no longer protects her. Whenever the gospel enters an environment, it prevails."

Erwin McManus, Mosaic Church

BREAKING THE CODE WILL LOOK differently in different places. Moreover, it is important to understand that code breaking is a process—a lifelong process. God has been at work in your life preparing you for the "moments" that will define who you are, and he will lead you to communicate with the people whom he has called you to reach. God will draw upon vast resources and values that he has built into your life to help you dream about and plan effective strategies. Trust him, seek him, and believe that he will lead you to discover the right people, insights, and tools to develop an effective code-breaking strategy. Also, remember that it is not going to happen all at once. You will discover insights as you engage in the process of gathering information and getting to know your community and its people. Do not think of code breaking as a destination.

There are many "tools" that can help us get started on this code-breaking journey. Volumes of books exist to assist international missionaries exegete tribal societies for the sake of the gospel. Few resources are available to help us do the same thing here in the States. Below is a list of guidelines that will help you with the process of breaking the code in the community to which God has called you. You may discover other helpful tools as you use and develop the ones listed below.

Understanding Self

There are many issues of self that must be addressed before addressing issues of mission. We believe that too many church leaders start or grow churches in their heads rather than their context. That leads to a monument, not a movement.

Confirm God's Call upon Your Life

Before anything else, you must be called to a community. We are convinced that a key problem in many churches and among their leaders is that they have not truly heard from God. They have not heard the call of God in a clear and compelling way and responded with "Lord, here I am, send me!"

Having a clear calling from God involves having a clear sense of biblical purpose in your life—a sense of holy destiny. It also relates to the passions and convictions that exist in your life. Have you meditated on Jesus' missional directives in the New Testament to the point that you are moved to act upon what he has spoken? In addition, having a clear calling means that you will have a developing sense of God's future design for your life and ministry. Do you have a sense of passion and conviction about where he is leading you and your church?

People and churches that have a clear sense of God's call upon their lives can answer questions like this: Can you identify particular passages in the Bible that God has used to speak to you about his design for your life and the life of your church? Can you give definite examples of answered prayer in relationship to God's direction for your life and the ministry of the church? Do other believers affirm God's call and direction in your life and the life of your church?

This is probably the most critical aspect of all that we have discussed. We need to have God-called leaders who are not just interested in being in the profession of ministry. We need God-called leaders who are passionate and ready to persevere in the ministry to which God calls them. Clarify and confirm God's calling upon your life and the ministry of your church.

Fall in Love with the People

You can never break the code in a community if you are not deeply in love with the community and its people. A healthy code-breaking church or leader loves the people and their community. We always notice that international missionaries truly love the culture where they live, often more than the culture back home. My friend, Tim Vaughn, explained it to me this way: "It's a strange thing—early on in our time of missionary service in Germany, the "German ways" seemed so very different and our thinking was often, "If they would only do things the Amercian way, then . . . ." After several years in Germany, we would come back for visits to the USA and suddenly the thinking was more, "If they would only do things the German way, then . . . ." Our children would not even eat the American bread. They called it *Luftbrot* (air bread). Now, having been stateside for almost seven years we find ourselves often speaking German, looking for German foods, trying to meet Germans. We have come to terms with the fact that a large part of who we are, what we think, and how we view things—a large part of our hearts—is now German!"

People like Tim criticize American culture because they love their new home. In a sense, that is how it should be with us. We need to love the culture where God sends us and not be longing for the way it was somewhere else.

Think about how Jesus demonstrated this concept. He took the time to walk and live among the people, to listen to and tell stories, to welcome the little children, and to recognize and meet people's needs. Jesus loved people so much that he was moved with deep compassion over how lost they were, and then he acted upon that compassion and demonstrated God's love in practical and various ways to comfort them in their pain, meet their desperate needs, and share in their joys.

You must care about the community if you are going to reach it. Scripture, which tells a story starting in a garden but ending in the city, tells us that the benefit of our community (in this case the city of Babylon) matters to God.

> This is what the LORD Almighty, the God of Israel, says to
> all those I carried into exile from Jerusalem to Babylon:
> "Build houses and settle down; plant gardens and eat what
> they produce. Marry and have sons and daughters; find
> wives for your sons and give your daughters in marriage,
> so that they too may have sons and daughters. Increase in
> number there; do not decrease. Also, seek the peace and
> prosperity of the city to which I have carried you into exile.
> Pray to the LORD for it, because if it prospers, you too will
> prosper" (Jer. 29:4–7).

For many churches, particularly in areas that some people consider undesirable, this is a hard step. Once they loved the people who lived around their church but somehow, somewhere along the way, things changed . . . and they have not yet fallen in love with the community that is around them now. We can never reach a community that we do not love. We will never reach people whom we are unwilling to love. If you are having a difficult time loving the community, pray. You must ask God to change your heart and the hearts of the people in your church! Once God softens our hearts toward the community, then we begin to live as aliens who love the community where God made us sojourners.

You should begin to care about the context in such a way that people in the community see your love and consider you an advocate. They speak of you as they did in Isaiah, "Your people will rebuild the ancient ruins and will raise up the age-old foundations; you will be called Repairer of Broken Walls, Restorer of Streets with Dwellings" (Isa. 58:12).

Die to Yourself and Your Preferences

Before anything that is truly of God can be born, your own preferences have to die. Your desire to lead a contemporary / traditional / emerging / casual / formal / whatever church has to be laid on the altar and sacrificed in order to receive Christ's call and mission to this community. That is what Jesus meant when he said to his disciples in Luke 9:23, "If anyone would come after me, he must deny himself and take up his cross daily and follow me."

It is believed that John Knox cried out to the Lord, "Give me Scotland or I shall die." A better missional prayer might be—"Lord, help me die to self so that I can reach Scotland." In essence, isn't that what Paul meant in 1 Corinthians 9:22–23: "To the weak I became weak, to win the weak. I have become all things to all men so that by all possible means I might save some. I do all this for the sake of the gospel, that I may share in its blessings." Paul was consumed with fulfilling God's call upon his life—reaching the Gentiles with the gospel of Jesus Christ. That was the guiding force and directive in his life.

Are you willing to die to your preferences so the people in your community can be reached with the gospel? Is your church willing to move out of its Christian subculture and relate to its community? Is it possible that you and your church are missing out on some of the blessings of the gospel because you have been unwilling to die to yourself and your preferences?

Examine Your Leadership Readiness

Until you know your leadership readiness, you will find countless excuses for why you cannot break the code. Often it is because you are unprepared and ill-equipped. We are often amazed as pastors tell us all the reasons they fail, but seldom do we hear, "I was just not ready."

Understanding Community

Get Counselors from the Context

Counselors from the context are not just the experts (though the experts are important). They are the people who live in the culture. Getting counselors from the context means making friends with people who are like the people group that you are trying to reach. It means taking the time to really get to know and understand the community and the people whom you are called to reach.

There are some simple ways to begin this process. You could invite some people over to your home for a casual meal or cookout. Another way to engage in this process is to search for the places where people "hang out"—coffee shops, fast-food restaurants, parks, etc. Just start hanging out with the people and getting to know them.

Identify Natural Barriers of Your Community

Are there interstate highways, rivers, or other natural boundaries that limit the interaction of the people in the area which God has provided you as a mission field? Start mapping them on a good map. Determine the main arteries that supply the area. Analyze how the locations of these arteries and barriers impact where your church might minister and meet.

Review the Census Information

Go to www.census.gov and get more information. This will help you identify various population segments and population shifts. You might discover critical information regarding increases or decreases within a particular area or people group that will become a key in building a missional approach.

Study Demographic Information

There are lots of good companies. We tend to use the study from the Leavell Center (www.leavellcenter.com). You can also contact your denominational agencies and see what kinds of resources they might have available to assist you or your church in this area.

It is important to study the demographic information about your community because it can reveal all kinds of helpful insights like age breakdowns, ethnic groups, and even people group characteristics. If you study recent demographic history and compare it to the current information, it can reveal important changes that have taken place in the community that might provide a key insight as you develop an effective outreach strategy.

Talk to the Experts

There are people in every community who know more than you know. And if you are truly going to reach a community, you need to become the expert. That means you need to make contacts with some of those people who know more than you do:
- local government officials,
- the local planning commission,
- school board members,
- the chamber of commerce,
- community service agencies,
- school teachers/administrators,
- policemen, and
- health care professionals.

In the process of planting Lake Ridge Church, our pastoral leadership team read a history of the county, started studying a map, and started talking to people. That is where every church can start: with a history book, map, and conversations. Here is a list of some questions that could be used when you talk to some of the experts in your community:

- What are the three best-kept secrets about this community?
- Who are three people that love this community and understand the people who live here (you want to talk to anybody who loves the community)?
- What changes do you see on the horizon for this community?
- What are some of the most significant events that have taken place in this community's history?
- Can you tell me any community needs that are going unmet in this area?

Move Beyond Demographics and Anecdotal Conversations

Drive around the area and see if the people you think are there are really in the area. You can do this by making observations from the car, but you should also get out and eat at the restaurants, shop at the local shops, and socialize at the local places. This is ultimately the only way to get a "feel" for the people and the community.

Do Prayer Walks

A prayer walk is simply what it says: walking (or driving) through a community while praying for the people. Ask God to reveal things to you as you walk. Here are specific things to request:

- Ask God to show you how to reach the people who live in the homes that you pass.
- Ask God to prepare people's hearts to receive his Word and draw them to Jesus Christ.
- Ask God to reveal a person of peace as you move around the area.

- Ask God to help you understand how you can meet practical needs in the community and show the love of Christ.

Identify Spiritual Strongholds

As you do the prayer walk, God will begin to reveal other things about which to pray—both things to stand against and things to affirm. Make spiritual warfare part of your strategy. Pray that God might reveal what keeps local people from trusting in Jesus Christ, and then ask the Holy Spirit to break through those barriers. The history and industry of the community may also provide insight regarding spiritual strongholds.

Review the History; Become the Expert

Ask some questions about the community. Here are some further questions that could be asked to discover important information about the community's history: What brought people here in the first place? Who moved in? When did they move in? Who is moving in now? How have things changed? What have been the leading industries in the past? As you study the history, look for points of connection that God can use to impact the culture.

Understanding Networks

"One must approach the task with the recognition that God is already at work in this community, and [my] task as a networker is to discover how He is at work."[1] Part of our job, as we exegete to understand our mission field, is to connect meaningfully with those who already are relationally invested in the community we are seeking to reach. That requires an intentional process.

Determine who influences the people that God has called you to reach. Ask who your people listen to—radio hosts, newspapers, politicians, etc. Begin to reach out to and listen to those influences and influencers. Make a point of connecting with them and introduce yourself to them. Pray for them. Determine whether any of these key influencers are believers and how you might be able to partner with them to impact your community. In addition, you can begin to use references to and illustrations from these sources in your sermons and during other teaching opportunities. That will help you connect with and reach your people group.

Find "Bridge People" from the Context. God has already placed people in the community whom he plans to use to transform the culture with the gospel. As we mentioned earlier, some of the best evangelists are those who need evangelizing themselves—people who have not yet committed to Christ but who are connected to others who need Christ. As a code-breaking church leader, your purpose is to discover bridge networks over which the gospel can travel.

You must look for people with already existing relational networks. Rather than connect with just anyone, you will focus on those who will have connections. What are "connections"? For this world's purposes connections are social and economic relationships. For the purpose of the gospel, connections are something different—connecting for the purpose of proclaiming the gospel among networks of people. Don't just build your own network; connect within the networks of others.

Understanding Where God Is Working in Churches and in Cultures

God is already working in your community. He is working through existing churches and in present culture. Existing churches probably already know much of what you need to discover. Ray Bakke explains, "I've done consultations in over 200 cities. When they ask for help, I'll say: 'Most of what you need to know is already in your city. Would you be willing to go ask every bishop in town, "If you had to prove God is alive in your city, what would you point to to prove it?" . . . My role has been interpreting the city from Scripture and history.'"[2]

God has already been at work in cultures, preparing people to hear the news of Jesus Christ. He has placed peoples entwined with metaphors, redemptive analogies, and passions. Your role is to find them, connect with them, and be Christ in their culture.

Find All the Churches in Your Area and Map Them Out

Make a list of all the churches of every kind. Add cults and sects to the map. If you can get the information, begin to map who is growing, who is not, and why. Find out if new churches have been planted in the area and what the results were.

Research Indigenous Churches

Contact churches that are already reaching people in your community. Some may already be indigenous to the people you are called to reach. Find out what they have done to connect with the community. Find out what they have already tried that failed. If you cannot find any in your immediate community, find some in a nearby (and similar) community.

Determine Their Musical Preferences

What music do the people in the community listen to? Do they listen to the same type of music for worship that they do in the culture? What are the top three radio stations for your focus group? Is a major musical style immoral even though it is enjoyed by a majority of people in the culture? Do existing Christians avoid certain styles for moral reasons? What musical styles are used by different indigenous churches?

Answering these questions will help you determine the kind of music that will fit best in your worship gatherings. It will also help you determine what kinds of instruments and musicians you might need to recruit.

Musical style and worship are not the same thing. Morgenthaler explains it well:

Time is running out for mere Band-Aids and face-lifts. All the technique in the world cannot produce worshipers. It cannot produce worship. The time has come to make technique the servant of spirit and truth. . . . Only then will we be able to engage believers in heartfelt, active response to a living God. Only then will our worship be genuinely attractive to the seeker who is hungering to see what a supernatural relationship with God is like. Only then will our worship produce the by-product God intended: a witness to Christ.[3]

We need to be worshipers, and figuring out music is not the answer to that. But, with the right heart, the right music becomes a tool to create biblically faithful and indigenous music.

Determine Their Dress

What do the people in the community wear? Do they dress up, down, or the same for special occasions? What do people wear at the growing churches in the area? This will help you discern what kind of environment you need to create in your worship gatherings—suit and tie, business casual, cowboy hats and boots, Hawaiian shirts and sandals, jeans and T-shirts, etc. What are indigenous churches doing, and what can we learn from them?

Determine Their Leadership Systems

Are the people used to a situation where leadership is centralized and clearly in charge (more blue collar factory workers), or are they more accustomed to participatory leadership (more white collar management)? How are the growing churches governed? These questions are critical if you are going to develop an effective organizational/leadership structure. If you choose a church governing system that correlates with the people group and their leadership systems, church life and church development can be much less stressful. Remember one size does not fit all. Scripture provides normative forms, but how these are applied in individual contexts is often a cultural issue.

Determine How They Learn

Do the people learn through mentoring relationships, in classroom settings, or in small groups? Do they learn in a modern "either/or" fashion or more of a postmodern "both/and" format? Do they transfer history, culture, and learning through storytelling or more of a structured lecture format? Answering these questions should influence the way that you communicate gospel truth with your focus group.

Addressing these issues will enable you to develop a culturally appropriate strategy as you are being led by the Holy Spirit. The steps are not the Holy Spirit. They are tools that provide information to help us determine the type of strategy that God will likely use in reaching different people groups. This process will help us break the unbroken code.

Identify the People Groups in the Area that Are Within Your Mission Context

If you have identified a specific area, find out who lives there— not just people like you or your focus group, but find out about everyone living in the area. The more you discover and learn about the people groups and community, the more effective you will become in relating to and communicating with all the people in your area. It is also likely that you will have many opportunities to minister to all kinds of people in your area (see www.peoplegroups.info for help). In addition, God may lead you to start other ministries or churches than your current one. Moreover, you may find groups similar to your focus group. Most importantly, God is already at work there.

Conclusion

It takes work to understand and reach a context. Most won't take the time, and they will never truly break through to impact their community. They will have lots of explanations and will spend their energy copying others or retying failed strategies, but they just can't convince themselves to change. They think, *What worked in Chicago, in the past, or in my head will work here—if we just try harder.*

Some will break the code without trying. God, in his sovereignty, will line up their cultures and gifts with those in the community and explosive things will occur. They won't know why it happened that way, but they will tell you to "do what I did . . . I just preached the Word and people came." You will never be able to convince most of them that God gave them a gift of alignment with their community and you need to figure out yours.

Some will take the time and energy required. Our prayer is that more will do so because of this book—and that they will proclaim Christ and impact lostness in a powerful way because they become missionaries in their communities.

The Breaking the Code Challenge

1. What specific passages of Scripture has God used to confirm and shape your calling to break the code?
2. How can you cultivate a love relationship with your community?
3. Describe the culture to which you are called to minister in terms of music, dress, leadership style, learning approaches, how people relate, etc.
4. Describe the culture within the church you need to create in order to effectively reach your community.

Chapter 16

Breaking the Unbroken Code

"To speed up my learning, I also took a part-time job at Starbucks. Since I had grown up as a pastor's kid, I thought I understood evangelism. But my three years at Starbucks taught me that simple formulas and canned presentations were woefully incomplete if we were to connect with this generation."

Daniel Hill, River City Community Church

MODERNITY IS OUT AND POSTMODERNITY is in! Well, that is mostly true. Perhaps it is more accurate to say that we are in a transition. As Benjamin Barber put it, "The planet is falling percipiently apart and coming together again at the very same moment."[1] A NetFax article described the transition this way:

We are living in the midst of two major shifts in human history. Both are not limited to the United States but are occurring worldwide. One is the shift from the Industrial Age to the Information Age and the other is the shift from the modern world to the postmodern world. Both shifts are "in process" and one reason we are experiencing such dissonance and apparent chaos is that we are in the "in-between times." The old is not yet fully dead and the new is not yet fully born.[2]

Just a few years ago in *How to Reach Secular People,* George Hunter was right when he summed up Diogenes Allen's observation by noting, "This means that the pillars of 'modern' western civilization, erected during the Enlightenment, are now crumbling. Allen observes that we are now in a period of culture lag—in which most people in the western world are not yet as aware as scientists and philosophers that the Enlightenment is over. But, Allen predicts, 'when the dust settles,' we will see that 'the fields are ripe for the harvest.'"[3] Now that the dust is settling, there is an incredible opportunity to break the unbroken code.

Eddie Gibbs reminds us that most are not breaking through: "Wherever we look throughout the Western world, there is no evidence to date that current renewal movements, including charismatic churches, mega churches, new paradigm/apostolic networks and new churches have been sufficiently influential to turn the tide in national churchgoing trends."[4]

In order for this code to be broken, we need to rethink North America in light of these radical shifts, and we must learn to navigate the missional waters on our own continent.

Breaking the Unbroken Code Requires That We No Longer See Missions and Evangelism as Two Separate Disciplines

Most of us grew up in a world that viewed missions and evangelism very differently. David Hesselgrave describes nineteenth-century missionary advances in the following way: "Mission took the form of establishing schools and hospitals, opposing inhumane practices . . . and launching campaigns for sanitation." While applauding the great sacrifices these missionaries made, he goes on to state: "We moderns have tended to perpetuate confusion at this point. We have multiplied parachurch missions as arms of the church in order to undertake every conceivable type of good work from feeding the hungry, to immunizing populations against disease, to introducing new strains of corn and cattle."[5]

On the other hand, "Evangelism became identified too closely with great campaigns or crusades designed to win individuals to a commitment to Jesus Christ."[6] The question becomes, "Where is the church?" Did Jesus Christ not institute the church as his missionary instrument for fulfilling the Great Commission? The heart of the Great Commission is to "make disciples." Earlier in this book, we described a disciple as one who lives like Jesus lived, loves like Jesus loved, and leaves behind what Jesus left behind. The entire gospel is about the life of Jesus and how he responded to the culture in which he lived. Paul goes a step further when he declares that we are "the body of Christ." Those things that Jesus began to do and teach, he continues today through the church. With that being said, it is impossible to separate missions and evangelism from the role of the local church.

We must consider two issues. First, *as we go to the world,* we must establish churches that will accept the call of Christ and the responsibility of the church to care for the whole nature of man. As Jesus stated when he quoted from Isaiah, "The Spirit of the Lord is on me, because he has anointed me to preach good news to the poor. He has sent me to proclaim freedom for the prisoners and recovery of sight for the blind, to release the oppressed, to proclaim the year of the Lord's favor" (Luke 4:18–19).

Second, *as the world comes to us,* we must open our arms in order to fulfill the Great Commission. This involves how we view the local church and our willingness to take responsibility for discipling those who are very different from us, and yet, they literally live at our back doors. Bringing missions and evangelism together means realizing that the church is the missionary, and it exists on the mission field.

As we have stated earlier, we can no longer view North America as a Christian nation. In *Planting New Churches in a Postmodern Age,* Ed wrote:

> "Christendom" has come to an end. No longer is Christianity the "chaplain" to the broader culture. Christianity was universally assumed as the American religion even though it was not widely embraced. It was once perceived as part of our national ethos. No longer can that claim be made. This "humiliation" of Christendom has been underway for two centuries. It is no longer appropriate, if it ever was, to speak of "Christian America."[7]

With this in mind, viewing the church as the missionary impacts the way we do church locally and the way we engage our context. When this happens, we open our doors to those who are yet to decide whether Christianity is a valid option. While they may be very spiritual in nature, they have yet to decide what "spirit" they are going to follow. This impacts every aspect of our local churches from the way we invite people to participate in our Christian community to the way we send people out to accomplish Jesus' mission.

As we give up our rights and privileges as followers and engage those outside of Christ, we become the missionaries of God. As the body of Christ, we recognize that our efforts are dependent upon the *whole* body. Therefore, the mission of the church to fulfill the Great Commission does not get relegated to a program of evangelism, but it becomes intricately woven through the entire fabric of the local church.

We engage our context by inviting those who are most like us into an environment of love and acceptance. It is important that this environment connects with them culturally. If it does not speak their language, address their needs, overcome their obstacles, and allow them to experience community and faith over a long period of time, they will likely move on to something other than the church.

On the other hand, we engage those whose cultural distinctives are beyond our reach by planting churches among them that speak their language. When the church is the missionary, this requires an intentional commitment and strategy for reaching people groups, population segments, and environments that are distant from the church. It is naive to think that any one church can be the kingdom of God for the entire community. Therefore, when the church sees itself as the missionary, it calls forth the best of the church in terms of partnership and cooperation. When the church of Jesus Christ functions as the missionary, it will not be content until there is a New Testament congregation within the reach of all people in its given context.

Breaking the Unbroken Code Requires that We Go to Unreached People

Tom Clegg and Warren Bird offer the church a sobering wake-up call when they state in their book *Lost in America:* "The way Christians do church today is the equivalent of ignoring millions of desperate, but unrecognized, cries for help. We're letting an increasing number of our neighbors and friends die without a personal exposure to the life-giving good news of Jesus Christ. Unless we make some drastic changes, many people are likely to perish, and we'll fail in the mission of what God has called us to become and do."[8]

While an analysis of many churches' databases prove this statement to be true, we are grateful at the same time for a movement of churches across North America that are willing to pay the high price required to reach unreached people.

Over the last two decades, we have seen an aggressive seeker movement across North America. This movement has done much to revitalize the North American church in the suburbs. However, there are still many unreached people living in North America with no culturally relevant church within walking or driving distance. For many of these groups of people, Christianity is not even on the radar screen as a valid option. As a result of this, there are several frontiers we must pay close attention to if we are going to break the code. We must leave the confines of our established churches and go into the "highways and hedges." Where are these "highways and hedges"? They are certainly not as well defined as they once were. However, there are some places that we need to begin our search.

Emerging Populations

For the most part, our children will most likely attend different churches than the ones we attend or start. This is true for us, and we have no reason to expect anything else. For the most part, each generation will require its own church that speaks its own language in its own style. If this is true for our children, it is certainly true for emerging populations that have no Christian background. The existing church must accept the responsibility for sending out its emerging leaders to pioneer new approaches to reaching their generation. We must empower our own children to become missionaries to their own generation.

1.5 and 2nd Generation Ethnicity

Upon first glance, it is easy for us to assume that because there is a church that ministers to a certain ethnicity that we have planted adequate seed for making disciples among that ethnic group. This is not necessarily the case. Even more so than our children, children of first-generation ethnic groups who grow up speaking their native language in their home and English outside their home are often disconnected from their first-generation churches. More often, they prefer to worship in English, while maintaining some of their cultural distinctives.

Among Those Who Are "Already" Spiritual

These adults and their children are very spiritual and open to faith, but not in the same way they were a few decades back. They are now "spiritual" but without a connection to biblical Christianity and the Holy Spirit.

We both had an encounter in Park City, Utah, a couple of years back that illustrates this point. While having lunch we began to have a conversation with our server. She was a young lady in her early twenties and quickly engaged in a conversation with us about spiritual issues. She informed us that she was in a house group that met and worshiped on a regular basis. With a little further probing, we realized that she was wiccan (although she did not actually know what that was).

We let her know that we too were in a group that met in a home and follow a man who claimed to be the Son of God and was named Jesus. We then told her about a book we studied called the Bible and how it had a part in the book known as the Gospels that would be a good starting point discovering more about this Jesus. She was very open to that gospel. This young lady represents a growing group of spiritually seeking people in North America.

Multihousing Dwellers

"Sixty percent of the unchurched population in North America (United States and Canada), some 120 million people, live in multi-housing communities."[9] The majority of these multihousing dwellers will remain unchurched and unreached unless groups and churches are planted within the confines of these unique communities. These multihousing communities represent one of the cultural environments that we have already referenced. For the most part, the code continues to go unbroken among mutihousing dwellers.

Urban Dwellers

There is no doubt that God knew our cities would play a vital role in breaking the code in the twenty-first century. According to Ray Bakke, "The more than 1,200 references to cities (in scripture) are but a starting point for understanding God's agenda in the city."[10] According to U.N. Secretary-General Kofi Annan, half (of) the world's population will live in cities in two years (2007).[11] Bakke goes on to suggest that "most of the world's unreached peoples are culturally rather than geographically distant from local churches; local urban churches and their pastors can be at the leading edge of cross-cultural international mission in our time . . . [but] the majority of churches and pastors are not ready for this mission."[12]

Obviously, there are many reasons we must seize the opportunity for breaking the code in our cities. Sheer population numbers and the lack of strength in our existing city churches only scratch the surface. In many ways, most unreached people groups, population segments, and cultural environments first find their way to the city. Yet the city is a hard field in which to sow. It may require incredible resources and years of hard work in order to break the code.

Collegians

A recent development in church planting is that of planting churches on or near college campuses. Leaders are discovering that when churches are planted on campus they are more strategic at reaching unreached and disconnected people on the college campus. They represent a shift from college and campus ministries that focus on those who already embrace the faith to that of planting the gospel among those who have never or seldom heard.

We could continue to expand upon this list of places that we need to get started. Literally hundreds of groupings of unreached people could be reached if there was a church for them. As we have implied throughout this book, we can no longer view North America simply through the lenses of people groups. We must now turn over every stone if we are to fulfill the Great Commission. This includes reaching out to the many emerging population segments and cultural environments. We must learn to see the hidden people of North America. We must prayerfully ask questions like: "Where are the unreached people?" "Who are the unreached people?" "Why are they unreached?" "What is being done to reach these people?" "What can I do to reach these people?"

Breaking the Unbroken Code Requires that We Empower Apostolic Leaders

In order to break the unbroken code, we must send apostolic leaders into the North American mission field to break the code! There was a day when we could argue that North America, or at least parts of it, were a harvest field in that people had a positive predisposition toward the gospel, and the church was poised to reach and receive these people. This is no longer the case. A "tending the store" mentality will not cut it. Hunter is right when he forces us to contrast the difference between now and then:

> By comparison, the earliest apostles and their colleague leaders and congregations saw their mission and mission field with pristine clarity. The recorded early traditions about the apostles leave no doubt about their job description. That tradition does not picture the apostles primarily as church administrators or desk theologians. Primarily each was "sent out" (*apostello* in the Greek) into the world by the Holy Spirit, usually a new field, area, or ethnic population to extend the Church to people groups who had not yet received the opportunity. That was their vocation: and their congregations, once planted, continued the outreach.[13]

Apostolic leaders in today's context are the missionary pioneers of previous days. They recognize that the church consists of those who are "sent out" into the harvest fields. They are the true pioneers of today. Breaking the code challenges us to rethink how we need to partner with these apostolic influencers. They force us to redefine the role of the church as a missionary church that is responsible for sending out apostles and lay apostles into the harvest field. If we are God's sent people, we must assume the responsibility to send out our best leaders into the field. Like Paul, we must imagine new ways of providing for and resourcing these apostolic leaders. We must rethink the role of the church in the local community and beyond.

Breaking the Unbroken Code Requires the Development of Learning Communities

In the mid-nineties, new learning communities began to spring up around the idea of this emerging postmodern culture. At a time when we were still trying to get our arms around the seeker movement, Leadership Network hosted a conference in Mt. Herman, California, that brought many different groups together to begin to examine the issues related to this major shift in our culture. Plenary sessions were held for early pioneers to present their findings in a cultural context fit for any person that claimed to be postmodern. After the plenary sessions, the larger groups were dispersed into smaller groups that were divided by affinity where specific questions were raised and discussed. Finally, new discoveries were submitted to the larger community. Bringing together those who are breaking the code can be affirming, but it can also facilitate the rapid acceleration of new thought and ideas related to breaking that specific code. That is a true learning community.

Connecting the dots is an important part of bringing these communities together. It is important for us to grasp that when the code has been broken among a certain people group, population segment, or cultural group (regardless of the distance these cultural groups may have geographically), they share many things in common. Of course, there will be many adaptations and differences, but there are also many similarities. This is good news for the apostolic leader. Because of this reality, specific strategies that connect the dots within existing movements can be implemented. It is essential that we report findings related to similar cultural groups, and then find ways to disperse those discoveries to those that are most likely to benefit from them.

Breaking the Unbroken Code Requires Preparing the Soil

Breaking the unbroken code requires that we prepare the fields for harvest. There are two types of fields when it comes to planting the gospel. There are harvest fields and there are sowing fields. There are still many harvest fields throughout the world. But more and more there are sowing fields. Sowing fields may often require years of hard work before we see any fruit. Often, we gauge our success by the harvest. In many cases, we will need to redefine success and impact.

One question the North American church must answer honestly is this, "Are we willing to invest the time required to break the code?" If so, we will have to avoid the temptation that comes from living in a consumer-oriented society of instant gratification. We are learning that those who take the time necessary to plow, sow, water, and prune can reap a harvest of souls, but this takes time. There was a time when the plowing, sowing, watering, and pruning were done for us. This is no longer the case.

This will require apostolic leaders spending years planting the gospel in a way that is safe and culturally close to various people groups, population segments, and cultural groups. When the gospel begins to take root, we must be prepared to plant churches. This apostolic pattern begins with the planting of the gospel. When the gospel is planted and disciples are made, then churches are established.

Breaking the Unbroken Code Requires Seeing North America through a Different Set of Lenses

We have said it over and over again, but we must continue to say it. Breaking the unbroken code requires that we see North America differently. Jesus saw the city and wept over it. He saw the crowds and said they were "white unto harvest." We must deploy apostolic leaders into the harvest to give us a realistic assessment of our mission field. Research will be an important tool as we move forward. We must continue to discover where the unreached people groups, population segments, and cultural environments are. We must also continue to assess their relationship in terms of the harvest. Along the way, when we see God at work, we must be quick to join him in this good work. Doing this will require us to prioritize the many unreached people of North America.

Breaking the Unbroken Code Requires Approaching North America on Our Knees

One of the mistakes we made in the past was beginning on our feet instead of our knees. Leaders who break the unbroken code make a commitment to begin on their knees—and lead their churches to do the same. Jesus reminded us of this reality in Matthew 9:35–38: "Jesus went through all the towns and villages, teaching in their synagogues, preaching the good news of the kingdom and healing every disease and sickness. When he saw the crowds, he had compassion on them, because they were harassed and helpless, like sheep without a shepherd. Then he said to his disciples, 'The harvest is plentiful but the workers are few. Ask the Lord of the harvest, therefore, to send out workers into his harvest field.'"

It seems to us that we are right back where we started. We face the same challenges Jesus did when he prayed this prayer. With this same challenge comes the same solution. "Ask the Lord of the harvest, therefore, to send out workers into his harvest field." Through prayer we see the harvest, and an army of code breakers can be mobilized. Through this we are reminded that we have everything we need to make a difference in a world that we are being sent into to "make disciples of all nations."

The Breaking the Code Challenge

1. What code remains unbroken within your community?
2. What will it take to break that code?
3. How do you turn your church into an army for breaking the unbroken code?

Epilogue

Unlike the previous notion of the church as an entity
located in a facility or in an institutional organization and
its activities, the church is being reconceived as a community, a gathered people, brought together by a common calling and vocation to be a *sent people*.[89]

Wayne started practicing as a chiropractor in the strip mall
where Summit Church was located. Summit Church was the church
I (David) planted where I learned much about breaking the code. It is
located near Charleston, South Carolina, and now meets on a college
campus. Wayne decided to attend the church because as he put it, "I
needed some new patients and thought church would be a good place
to get them." After the service Wayne thanked me and said, "What
you said today got into the trap door of my soul." After that Wayne
was hooked. He came every week.

Wayne grew up on Long Island, New York, where he attended a
good Catholic school. He decided organized religion was not for him
after he was disciplined for questioning issues related to faith. He had
not been to church in years.

One week I (David) preached about the exclusivity of Christ. After the service Wayne asked if we could meet during the week. During lunch that week we talked about the claims of Christ as the one and only way, and I presented the gospel to Wayne as clearly as I knew how. I will never forget his response: "David, do you think it is OK if I believe in God, but not Jesus Christ?"

I wanted to protest, but I sensed that it was O.K. if he remained open to the idea of Jesus as the one and only way. I told Wayne I thought that would be a great starting point, but I asked for permission to pray for him in that if Jesus was the one and only way that this God he could believe in would reveal this truth to him. He agreed and I prayed for him on the spot.

Over the next few months Wayne continued to attend church weekly and have coffee with me on a daily basis. He built relationships, got involved in many aspects of community within the church, and asked hundreds of questions. Finally one weekend he approached me and told me that he was going to take the weekend to go off with his wife and process all that he had been experiencing. When he returned, he dropped by to tell me that he had invited Jesus into his life as God's unique Son and the one and only way to heaven.

Jack was an Army helicopter pilot who started to visit a church that I (Ed) was starting. He was attending medical school, and we began to build a relationship. Our church did not have Sunday services yet, but he came to everything our "prelaunch" church planned. He wanted to be a part of our community. He was part of our core group without yet having a relationship to Christ.

He came because it was different from the religious world he had experienced in the past. He had been to a few churches but found that he could not ask his questions or think through his doubts.

It took Jack eighteen months of being a part of our community before he was ready to take that step of faith. Of course, he asked me a lot of questions on the way. One of my favorites was if he had to give up football to follow Christ (the games were played on Sunday, after all). Jack considered the claims of the Christ and the lives of Christ's followers for eighteen months, until he unceremoniously came by my office and announced, "I'm ready." He moved from a "seeker in community" to a "Christ follower" that day (or perhaps a long time before).

There was a time when people like Wayne and Jack represented the minority. Sure, there are still many people who fit and thrive within a church culture. Churches in certain places can survive and thrive even while ignoring people like Wayne, but no church can be faithful to the Great Commission and ignore such people. Soon our playing field will more and more consist of people like Wayne and Jack.

Today, we have to engage people in new ways. We have to remind and revision what a missional church looks like—a church sent to people in culture to share the risen Christ. "Follow me and I will make you fish for people" was the challenge Jesus gave the Galilean fishermen. *Following* and *fishing* are inseparably linked.[2] We need to engage people in both.

Churches that are going to break the code recognize and thrive on the idea of creating a context where people can experience the gospel. In addition to people like Wayne and Jack, code-breaking churches recognize that there are people like Jose, Lee, Rho, and the list goes on. Not only does everyone deserve to hear the gospel in their own cultural language, but they also deserve to experience the gospel in a safe place. This is the task we must commit ourselves to as the church of North America. Breaking the code is a noble call. Breaking the code is what we must give ourselves to if the church is to thrive in our emerging missional context. Breaking the missional code is our calling.

Endnotes

Introduction

1. Reggie McNeal, *The Present Future* (San Francisco: Jossey-Bass, 2003), 51.
2. Mark Mittelberg, *Building a Contagious Church* (Grand Rapids: Zondervan, 2001), 34.

Chapter 1: The Emerging Glocal Context

1. Parts of here and following are adapted from *Planting New Churches in a Postmodern Age.*
2. Craig Van Gelder, *The Essence of the Church* (Grand Rapids: Baker Books, 2000), 98.
3. Wilbert R. Shenk, *Write the Vision* (Harrisburg, Pa.: Trinity Press International, 1995), 43.
4. http://www.christianitytoday.com/ct/2002/100/33.0.html.
5. http://www.barna.org/FlexPage.aspx?Page=BarnaUpdateBarriw&aBarnaUpdateID=163.
6. http://www.marriagesavers.org/public/born_agains_have_high_divorce_ra.htm.
7. http://www.christianitytoday.com/ct/2005/001/26.42.html.
8. http://www.gallup.com/poll/content/?ci=7759.
9. See book review at http://www.nimblespirit.com/html/spiritual_but_not_religious_re.htm.
10. http://www.ivyjungle.org/GenericPage/DisplayPage.aspx?guid=34D65C35-D0A1-484B-8101-825040769623.
11. http://www.newsong.net/about/our_story.php
12. http://www.newsong.net/about/pressreleases/christianityToday_1204.php
13. http://www.ethnicharvest.org/ideas/m-america/EAN2201S.ppt.
14. http://www.ethnicharvest.org/ideas/m-america/EAN2201S.ppt.
15. http://www.matador.recs.com/survey/def_psycho.html.
16. http://www.campuschurch.net/about/about.php?go=history.

Chapter 2: Breaking the Missional Code

1. http://www.pastors.com/pcom/specials/rickbio.asp.

2. http://www.christianitytoday.com/workplace/articles/issue10-leanchurch.html.

3. Thanks to my (Ed's) copastor, Philip Nation, at Lake Ridge Church who contributed to this part. While I want to focus on the "work of the Lord," he reminds me to first focus on the "Lord of the work."

4. Rick Warren, *The Purpose Driven Church* (Grand Rapids: Zondervan, 1995), 191–92.

5. Ibid., 194.

6. Ibid.

7. Ibid., 155–72.

8. Michael Slaughter with Warren Bird, *UnLearning Church: Just When You Thought You Had Church All Figured Out* (Loveland, CO: Group Publishing, 2002), 15.

9. http://www.theaterchurch.com/CC_Content_Page/ 0,,PTID325928|CHID719468|CIID,00.html

Chapter 3: Engaging Community for Christ: The Commissions of Jesus

1. Dino Senesi, personal e-mail, July 10, 2005.

Chapter 4: The Missional Church Shift

1. Parts of this chapter and chapter 5 are adapted and excerpted with permission from *OnMission* magazine, North American Mission Board, SBC.

2. http://www.purposedriven.com/en-US/AboutUs/WhatIsPD/ 12+PD+Characteristics.htm.

3. http://www.catapultmagazine.com/02_04/article.cfm?issue=20&article=197.

4. Email from George Barna to Ed Stetzer, December 19, 2005.

Chapter 5: Transitions to Missional Ministry

1. Eddie Gibbs, *ChurchNext* (Downers Grove, Ill.: InterVarsity Press, 2000), 39.

2. www.apostles-raleigh.org.

3. Dino Senesi, e-mail, June 5, 2005.

Chapter 6: Values of Leaders and Churches That Break the Code

1. Jonathan Campbell, "Postmodernism: Ripe for a Global Harvest—But Is the Church Ready?" *Evangelical Missions Quarterly*, Vol. 35, No. 4, 1999. http://bgc.gospelcom.net/emis/1999/postmodern3.htm.

2. Michael Slaughter with Warren Bird, *UnLearning Church: Just When You Thought You Had Church All Figured Out* (Loveland, Colo.: Group Publishing, 2002), 26.

3. http://www.organicchurchplanting.org/about/mission.asp.

4. http://www.organicchurchplanting.org/articles/cma_movement.asp.

5. George G. Hunter, III, *How to Reach Secular People* (Nashville: Abingdon Press, 1992), 86.

6. Ibid., 85–88.

7. Reggie McNeal, *The Present Future: Six Tough Questions for the Church* (San Francisco: Jossey-Bass, 2003), 11.

8. Harvie M. Conn, *A Clarified Vision for Urban Mission* (Grand Rapids: Zondervan, 1987), 217.

Chapter 7: Contextualization: Making the Code Part of Your Strategy

1. Stuart Murray-Williams, "Emerging churches in post-Christendom," http://www.emergingchurch.info/reflection/stuartmurray-williams/.

2. http://www.christianitytoday.com/ct/2003/106/22.0.html

4. Dan Kimball, *The Emerging Church* (Grand Rapids: Zondervan, 2003), 186.

5. Ibid., 173. We change Dan's comment about "deconstructing" after talking with Dan. His concern is "gospel" as a musical style and *Armageddon* as a movie. Thus, the words need to be explained and defined anew.

6. Leonard Sweet, Brain D. McLaren, and Jerry Haselmayer, *The Language of the*

Emerging Church (Grand Rapids: Zondervan, 2003), 115–17.

Chapter 8: Emerging Strategies

1. Dave Travis, "Multiple-Site/Multiple-Campus Churches," Report from a Leadership Network Forum, September 11–12, 2001. www.leadnet.org.

2. Warren Bird, "Extending Your Church to More Than One Place: A Field Report on the Emerging Multi-Site Movement," Leadership Network, leadnet.org, June 2003, 4.

3. Warren Bird, quoting Elmer Towns, *Ten of Today's Most Innovative Churches* (Regal, 1990), 239. Although the book is out of print, it is available at www. elmertowns.com currently at no charge.

4. Mike Steele, personal conversation, April 6, 2005.

5. Wayne Grudem, *Systematic Theology: An Introduction to Biblical Doctrine* (Grand Rapids: Zondervan, 1994), 857.

6. "The Church," http://www.sbc.net/bfm/bfm2000.asp.

7. http://community.gospelcom.net/lcwe/assets/LOP43_IG14.pdf. Lausanne Occasional Paper No. 43, "The Realities of the Changing Expression of the Church," September 29—October 5, 2004, 23–25.

8. Ibid., 27–28.

9. Hunter, 83–84.

Chapter 9: Spiritual Formation and Churches that Break the Code

1. George G. Hunter, III, *How to Reach Secular People* (Nashville: Abingdon Press, 1992), 41.

Chapter 10: : Revitalization of Missional Ministry

1. http://www.onmission.com/site/c.cnKHIPNuEoG/b.830521/k.D281/Stirring_the_waters.htm.

Chapter 12: Emerging Networks: New Paradigms of Partnership

1. http://www.christianitytoday.com/ct/2004/005/4.36.html.

2. Mark Driscoll, Acts 29 Strategic Plan, March 15, 2005.

3. Glenn Smith, GlocalNet Update, e-mail, November 25, 2003.

4. Mark Driscoll, Acts 29 Strategic Plan, March 15, 2005.

5. Curtis Sergent, personal conversation, December 8, 2004.

6. http://www.pastors.com/RWMT/?artid=8139&id=200.

7. http://www.saddlebackfamily.com/peace/Services/110203_high.asx.

8. Lyle E. Schaller, *A Mainline Turnaround: Strategies for Congregations and Denominations* (Nashville: Abingdon Press, 2005), 18.

9. Ibid., 19.

10. Ibid., 74.

Chapter 13: Breaking the Code without Compromising the Faith

1. Darrell L. Guder, ed., *Missional Church: A Vision for the Sending of the Church in North America* (Grand Rapids: Eerdmans, 1998), 18.

2. Richard J. Mouw, "The Missionary Location of the North American Churches," in *Confident Witness—Changing World*, ed. Craig Van Gelder (Grand Rapids, Eerdmans, 1999), 8.

3. William J. Larkin, "Mission in Acts," in *Mission in the New Testament*, ed. William J. Larkin, Jr., and Joel F. Williams (Maryknoll, N.Y.: Orbis Books, 1998), 180.

4. Lesslie Newbigin, *A Word in Season* (Grand Rapids: Eerdmans, 1994), 67.

5. Paul McKaughan, Dellana O'Brien, and William O'Brien, *Choosing a Future for U.S. Missions* (Monrovia, Calif.: MARC, 1998), 22.

Chapter 14: Best Practices of Leaders and Churches that Break the Code

1. Reggie McNeal, *The Present Future: Six Tough Questions for the Church* (San

Francisco: John Wiley and Sons, Inc., 2003), 1.

2. Eddie Gibbs, *ChurchNext: Quantum Changes in How We Do Ministry* (Downers Grove, Ill.: IVP, 2000), 72.

3. McNeal, *The Present Future*, 8.

4. Rick Warren, *The Purpose Driven Church* (Grand Rapids: Zondervan, 1995), 190–91.

5. Andy Stanley, Reggie Joiner, and Lane Jones, *7 Practices of Effective Ministry* (Sisters, Oreg.: Multnomah, 2004), 140.

6. McNeal, *The Present Future*, i.

7. Lynne and Bill Hybels, *Rediscovering Church* (Grand Rapids: Zondervan, 1995), 44.

8. Jim Collins, *Good to Great* (New York: Harper Collins Publishers, 2001), 41–64.

9. http://www.vintagefaith.com/whatis.html.

10. Ibid.

11. Andy Stanley, Reggie Joiner, and Lane Jones, *7 Practices of Effective Ministry* (Sisters, Oreg.: Multnomah, 2004), 10–11.

12. Henry and Richard Blackaby, *Spiritual Leadership* (Nashville: Broadman & Holman, 2001), 69.

13. http://cpforum.net/cgi-bin/processrequest.cgi?action=display article&fromlist=true&articleid=265.

Chapter 15: The Process of Breaking the Code

1. Robert Linthicum, "Networking: Hope for the Church in the City." Urban Mission 4 (Jan 1987), 32–51.

2. http://cityvoices.gospelcom.net/pages/raybakke/ray_apstle.html.

3. Sally Morgenthaler, *Worship Evangelism* (Grand Rapids: Zondervan, 1996), 31.

Chapter 16: Breaking the Unbroken Code

1. William Easum, *Dancing with Dinosaurs: Ministry in a Hostile and Hurting World* (Nashville: Abingdon Press, 1993).

2. NetFax, number 46, May 27 1996.

3. George G. Hunter, III, *How to Reach Secular People* (Nashville: Abingdon Press, 1992), 38.

4. Eddie Gibbs, *ChurchNext: Quantum Changes in How We Do Ministry* (Downers Grove, Ill.: IVP, 2000), 80.

5. David J. Hesselgrave, *Planting Churches Cross-culturally* (Grand Rapids: Baker, 2000), 25.

6. Ibid., 26.

7. Ed Stetzer, *Planting New Churches in a Postmodern Age* (Nashville: Broadman and Holman, 2003), 14.

8. Tom Clegg and Warren Bird, *Lost in America* (Loveland, Colo.: Group: 2001), 15.

9. Kim Jude, "A Church Could Be Their Own," OnMission.com, an online publication for North American Mission Board, November–December, 2002.

10. Ray Bakke, "Planting and Growing Urban Churches," in *The Challenge of World Evangelization to Mission Strategy* (Grand Rapids: Baker, 1997), 80.

11. http://www.noticias.info/Archivo/2005/200502/20050218/20050218_48782.shtm.

12. Raymond J. Bakke, "Profiles of Effective Urban Pastors," in *Discipling the City*, 126.

13. Hunter, *How to Reach Secular People*, 108–9.

Epilogue

1. Darrell L. Guder, ed., *Missional Church: A Vision for the Sending of the Church in North America* (Grand Rapids: Eerdmans, 1998), 81.

2. Eddie Gibbs, *ChurchNext* (Downers Grove, Ill.: InterVarsity Press, 2000), 56.